D0851287

Fairy Tales for Two Readers

Fairy Tales for Two Readers

Adapted by

BETTY L. CRISCOE
and
PHILIP J. LANASA, III

TEACHER IDEAS PRESS
A Division of
Libraries Unlimited, Inc.
Englewood, Colorado
1995

This book is dedicated
with much love and appreciation
to our children, Amy Elizabeth and John Philip.

✠　✠　✠

TEACHER IDEAS PRESS
A Division of Libraries Unlimited, Inc.
P.O. Box 6633
Englewood, CO 80155-6633
1-800-237-6124

Library of Congress Cataloging-in-Publication Data

Criscoe, Betty L., 1940-
    Fairy tales for two readers / adapted by Betty L. Criscoe and
Philip J. Lanasa III.
        xii, 121 p. 22x28 cm.
        Includes bibliographical references (p. 119).
        ISBN 1-56308-293-4
        1. Oral reading. 2. Fairy tales. I. Lanasa, Philip J.
    II. Title.
    LB1573.5.C75   1995
    649'.58--dc20   95-7601
                                                         CIP

Contents

Acknowledgments

The stories in this book were adapted from the following sources:

"The Brave Little Tailor," "Clever Elsie," "The Cunning Little Tailor," and "Mother Holly" were adapted from *The Complete Grimm's Fairy Tales* by Jakob L. K. Grimm and Wilhelm K. Grimm. Copyright © 1944 by Pantheon Books and renewed 1972 by Random House, Inc. Adapted by permission of Pantheon Books, a division of Random House, Inc.

"Cap O' Rushes," "Kate Crackernuts," "Mr. and Mrs. Vinegar," "The Black Bull of Norroway," "Chicken Little," and "The Three Pigs" were adapted from *English Fairy Tales* by Joseph Jacobs. Copyright © 1967.

"The Goose Girl," "King Thrushbeard," "The Seven Ravens," "The Six Servants," and "The Turnip" were adapted from fairy tales written by the Brothers Grimm.

Introduction

This book, which contains fifteen adapted fairy tales, was prepared for those who need to practice oral reading. The stories are arranged in dialogue format for two readers. Rehearsal involved in the paired experience is reading practice with a purpose.

Background of
Fairy Tales for Two Readers

After struggling through required oral reading practice with our own son, we became aware of the need for this kind of oral reading script. As parents, it was painful to sit passively by and listen as he struggled to master pronunciation and gain meaning from each fifteen-minute session of oral reading. It occurred to us that we needed a script for two readers, a script that would allow us to become actively involved in the oral reading practice and make reading aloud fun. Because of his new interest, our son was motivated to master his part and our part as well. Soon we found that he was reading both parts of the script smoothly, without pronunciation errors, and with meaning.

Teachers in our college classrooms were asked to use the stories in their classrooms, and they found the fairy tale scripts strengthened a variety of reading skills. The scripts provided good oral exercises in comprehension. In addition, a student who had to read the dialogue of Reader 1 also had to follow what the other student was reading, following the intonation, mood, and tone for each character. Teachers also found the scripts useful in training children to listen carefully. Teachers reported that the practice involved in mastering the fairy tale scripts helped students read more fluently, increasing students' enjoyment of reading and motivating them to read more. As students read orally, the teacher had an opportunity to informally observe the fluency, word identification, and comprehension skills of their students.

Teachers indicated they felt participating in paired reading activities helped their students become more sensitive to language styles and usage. They became more aware of the connection between print and spoken language. Students learned there are different ways of saying the same thing, each way relating to context as well as to the speaker's motivation.

Intended Audience

The fairy tales included in this compilation may be used by a parent and a child, a teacher and a child, or two children, one of whom reads slightly better than the other. These stories are at a reading level appropriate to children in the last half of the first grade and above. These high interest/low readability materials are appropriate for children who are past the stage of learning to read and who are secure enough in their word recognition ability to read to learn.

The stories are especially suited to older readers—remedial, corrective, or reluctant readers—who are having trouble phrasing, comprehending, and reading fluently aloud. These readers can direct their undivided attention to interpretation of character roles and use their skills of interpretation to search for personal meaning in the characters and situations. As readers interpret, think critically and creatively, read between the lines to make inferences, and experiment with each character's language, they transform printed language into expressive language that communicates thought and feeling.

The scripts may also be used by a child and an adult who appreciates having suitable material to read with children, who wants to encourage children to read better, or who would like to model good oral reading.

Reading Levels

Because the readability level of one of the parts is generally slightly more difficult than the other, the more difficult part should be read by the more capable reader. Students may not necessarily know all of the words the first time they read through the fairy tale scripts. Stress that students should read each script several times, ask for help pronouncing unknown words, and consult the glossary at the end of the story. A guide to the readability level of each story is provided in appendix A. Students should also evaluate their own reading by asking themselves the questions in the guide to oral reading in appendix B.

Tips for
Teachers and Parents

Teachers or parents should first read the story introduction to the student(s). They should call attention to the glossary at the end of each story, and time should be spent talking about words that might be difficult for the students. Students should first read the assigned fairy tale silently before reading it aloud to ensure that they have mastered word recognition and word meaning.

Next, the two participants should practice reading the fairy tale script aloud, without memorizing it. Eventually readers can perform for others in the class in informal groups. Encourage children to work on reading fluidly and with expression. Repeated reading provides additional oral reading practice and enables readers to improve their expression and characterizations. Once the oral reading has been mastered, participants might like to tape record or videotape their polished performances.

Values of Oral Reading

Research supports the use of reading aloud as a means of improving reading ability. The research of Carver and Hoffman (1981) suggests that poor readers who have decoding problems benefit from repeated oral reading. Leinholdt (1989) found reading aloud improved intonation, speaking skills, word recognition, reading rate, and comprehension, while boosting self-confidence. The research of Reutzel, Hollingsworth, and Eldredge (1994); Stallings (1980); and Wilkinson, Waldrop, and Anderson (1988) suggests that the time students spend in oral reading may be more directly tied to better reading attainment than silent reading.

Hoskisson, Sherman, and Smith (1974) suggest assisted reading as one technique for parents to help children overcome reading difficulties. Gautrey (1988) describes and evaluates a program based on paired reading. The program increased parents' involvement, while boosting childrens' reading ability and attitude toward reading.

As Graves and others indicate in their text, *Essentials of Classroom Teaching: Elementary Reading* (1994), "fluent oral reading is an indication of understanding . . . [and] reading aloud reinforces the concept that print represents words that have previously been familiar only in their spoken form." In addition, fluent oral reading is a valuable communication skill.

Values of Fairy Tales

Fairy tales have been created over centuries and yet have always addressed contemporary issues and values. Using fairy tales for oral reading practice provides several values:

1. These stories reflect many of the basic human needs, desires, and emotions that have remained unchanged through the ages. "Cap O' Rushes" shows the human need for acceptance and understanding. Like Clever Elsie, we all want the best for the future, and like her parents, we all want only the best for our loved ones. Fairy tales are built around the human need for security, love, and achievement.

2. Ethical truths are inherent in fairy tales. The humble and the good are exalted in "The Goose Girl," and in "Mother Holly," virtue is rewarded and selfishness is punished.

3. Readers of fairy tales can better understand the differences and common characteristics of people of different nationalities. The stories help children to see inside a culture, although reading fairy tales should never be substituted for the study of the culture.

Fairy tales are also very versatile. Because there are so many different types of fairy tales—animal tales, tales of magic, religious and romantic tales, tales of the stupid ogre, tales of pranksters and tricksters, and humorous anecdotes—one can find a story for any setting or mood. Also, the stories are filled with action and are suitable for all ages.

References

Carver, R. P., and J. V. Hoffman. "The Effect of Practice Through Repeated Reading in Gains in Reading Ability Using a Computer-Based Instructional System." *Reading Research Quarterly* 16, no. 3 (1981): 374-90.

Gautrey, Frances. "Paired Reading in a Middle School." *Reading* 22, no. 3 (November 1988): 175-79.

Graves, Michael F., Susan Watts, and Bonnie Graves. *Essentials of Classroom Teaching: Elementary Reading Method.* Boston: Allyn & Bacon, 1994.

Hoskisson, K., T. M. Sherman, and L. L. Smith. "Assisted Reading and Parent Intervention." *The Reading Teacher* 27 (1974): 710-14.

Leinholdt, L. M. "They Can All Sound Good." *Reading Horizons* 29, no. 2 (Winter 1989): 117-22.

Reutzel, D. R., P. M. Hollingsworth, and J. L. Eldredge. "Oral Reading Instruction: The Impact on Student Reading Development." *Educational Researcher* 29 (1994): 41-62.

Stallings, J. A. "Allocated Academic Learning Time Revisited, or Beyond Time on Task." *Educational Researcher* 9, no. 11 (1980): 11-16.

Wilkinson, I., J. L. Waldrop, and R. C. Anderson. "Silent Reading Considered: Reinterpreting Reading Instructions and Its Effects." *American Educational Research Journal* 25 (1988): 127-44.

FAIRY
TALES

The Black Bull of Norroway

Story Introduction

"The Black Bull of Norroway" is a romantic tale that has been adapted from one of Joseph Jacobs's English fairy tales. The main characters, a beautiful maiden and a fearless knight, are separated for seven long years through magic spells. Once they find each other, they must overcome the magic power of a witch to be together.

Reader 1:

Once upon a time there was a woman who had three daughters. The family lived in the northern part of England near the border of Scotland. One day the oldest daughter said to her mother . . .

Reader 2:

"Mother, bake me a bannock and roast me a collop. I am going away to seek my fortune!"

Reader 1:

"My daughter, I will do as you ask, but I am sad to see you go. You're my firstborn."

Reader 2:

The daughter went down the road to see the wise, old washerwife. She told the washerwife that she was on her way to find her fortune.

Reader 1:

"You stay with me a while. Look out the back door every day to see what you can see," said the washerwife.

Reader 2:

The first day the daughter saw nothing. The second day she saw nothing. The third day, when she looked out, she saw a coach drawn by six horses coming down the road. She ran to tell the washerwife.

Reader 1:

"That one's for you!" said the old woman.

Reader 2:

The daughter climbed into the coach. Off the horses galloped.

Reader 1:

Meanwhile, back home the second daughter approached her mother.

Reader 2:

"Mother, bake me a bannock and roast me a collop. It's time for me to seek my fortune," said the second daughter.

Reader 1:

"My daughter, I will do as you ask, but I am sad to see you go," said the mother.

Reader 2:

The mother helped the second daughter prepare for her journey. She, too, went to the old washerwife's house. She told the wise woman she was on her way to find her fortune.

Reader 1:

"You stay with me a while. Look out the back door every day to see what you can see," said the washerwife.

Reader 2:

The first day the second daughter saw nothing. The second day she saw nothing. On the third day, she saw a coach-and-four coming down the road.

Reader 1:

"That one's for you! Hurry and get on," said the old washerwife.

Reader 2:

The second daughter climbed into the coach. Down the road the coach went. In the meantime, the third daughter, who was back home, decided she wanted to leave and seek her fortune. She also went to see the old washerwife.

Reader 1:

"You stay with me a while. Look out my back door every day to see what you can see," said the wise woman.

Reader 2:

The first day the third daughter saw nothing. The second day she saw nothing. On the third day she looked again. There was a great black bull coming down the road.

Reader 1:

"That one's for you," said the old washerwife.

Reader 2:

The third daughter was full of grief and terror. Nevertheless, the old washerwife lifted the daughter up on the back of the great black bull. Away they went!

Reader 1:

Far they travelled. The young woman grew faint with hunger. Finally the bull said to her, "Eat out of my right ear. Drink out of my left ear. Leave what you can't eat."

Reader 2:

The damsel did as she was told. She was wonderfully refreshed by the food and drink. Long they rode. Hard they rode. Finally they came in sight of a fine castle.

Reader 1:

"We'll spend the night here with my oldest brother," said the black bull.

Reader 2:

The oldest brother lifted the young woman off the bull's back and then led her into the house. The bull was sent away to the field for the night.

Reader 1:

When it was morning, the brother took the young woman into a fine, shining parlor. He gave her a beautiful apple. He told her not to break the apple until she was in great danger.

Reader 2:

The brother then lifted the young woman onto the bull's back. Down the road the bull and the damsel went, far and hard. As night fell, they came in sight of a castle that was prettier than the first.

Reader 1:

"We'll spend the night here with my second brother," said the bull.

Reader 2:

The servants lifted the young woman off the bull's back and took her into the castle. They sent the bull away to the field for the night.

Reader 1:

In the morning the young woman was invited into a fine, rich room. She was given a beautiful pear and told not to break it until she was in serious trouble. Then the servants set her on the bull's back. Away went the bull and the damsel.

Reader 2:

They travelled far and hard. Finally they came in sight of the largest castle of all. "We'll stay in that castle tonight. My youngest brother lives there," said the black bull.

Reader 1:

At once the servants lifted the young woman down from the bull's back and walked with her into the castle. The bull was sent to the field for the night.

Reader 2:

The next morning the youngest brother took her into the finest room of all. He gave her a plum. He told her not to break it until she was in grave danger.

Reader 1:

The servants set the young woman on the bull's back. Away went the bull and the third daughter.

Reader 2:

On they rode until they came to a dark, ugly glen. There they stopped. The damsel got down from the bull's back.

Reader 1:

"Here you must stay while I go and fight the Old One. I must beat the Old One in order to remove the spell that has turned me into the form of a bull. Seat yourself on that stone. Move neither hand nor foot until I come back. If you move, I'll never find you again. If everything around you turns blue, you will know I have beaten the Old One. If everything turns red, that will mean the Old One has beaten me," said the bull.

From *Fairy Tales for Two Readers*. © 1995. Teacher Ideas Press. (800) 237-6124.

Reader 2:

The damsel set herself down on the stone. By and by all around her turned blue. She was very happy. She lifted one of her feet and crossed it over the other!

Reader 1:

As soon as the bull beat the Old One, the spell was indeed broken. The prince, who was no longer a bull, hurried back to look for the young woman. Alas, he could not find her!

Reader 2:

Long she sat, and long she wept until she was weary. Finally she rose and went away.

Reader 1:

She wandered until she came to a great hill of glass. She tried with all her might to climb the glass hill, but she couldn't. She walked around the bottom of the hill, sobbing and seeking a way over.

Reader 2:

Finally she came to a smith's house. The smith promised if she would serve him for seven years, he would make her a pair of iron shoes, and then she would be able to climb over the hill.

Reader 1:

At the end of seven years, the young woman had earned her iron shoes. Then she climbed the glass hill. She found herself at the door of another washerwife, but this one was really a witch!

Reader 2:

The old witch washerwife told the young woman about a gallant young knight who had once been a bull. He had given her some bloody clothes to wash. The person who could wash those bloody clothes clean would become the knight's wife.

Reader 1:

The old witch washerwife and her daughter had scrubbed until they were tired. They could not remove even one stain. They set the strange young woman to work. As soon as she began washing the clothes, all the stains came out, and the clothes became pure and clean.

Reader 2:

The old witch made the knight believe it was her daughter who had washed the clothes. So, the knight and the witch's daughter were to be married.

Reader 1:

The young woman was terribly upset! She knew the knight was the prince who had been a bull, and she loved him. She thought about her apple. Immediately she broke it. She found it filled with gold and precious jewelry, the prettiest jewelry she had ever seen!

Reader 2:

The young woman said to the witch's daughter, "All this gold and precious jewelry will I give to you if you will put off your marriage for one day. Allow me to go into the knight's room alone tonight."

Reader 1:

The false bride agreed. Then the old witch washerwife prepared a sleeping drink. She gave it to the knight who drank it. The knight slept until the next morning.

Reader 2:

All night long the damsel sobbed and sang, "Seven long years I served for thee. The glassy hill I climbed for thee. Thy bloody clothes I wrang for thee. Wilt thou not wake and turn to me?"

Reader 1:

The next day the damsel was so sad and disappointed. She broke the pear. It was filled with jewelry far richer than that in the apple. She used the jewelry to bargain with the witch's daughter for a second night in the knight's chamber.

Reader 2:

The old witch washerwife gave the knight another sleeping drink.

Reader 1:

Again he slept until morning.

Reader 2:

All night the damsel kept sighing and singing, "Seven long years I served for thee. The glassy hill I climbed for thee. Thy bloody clothes I wrang for thee. Wilt thou not wake and turn to me?"

Reader 1:

Still the knight slept. The damsel nearly lost hope altogether.

Reader 2:

The next day, while the knight was out hunting, a member of his hunting party asked him what the noises were coming from his bed chamber.

Reader 1:

Of course, the knight had heard no noises, but he decided to keep watch on the third night.

Reader 2:

The young woman was between hope and despair. This would be her last chance to win the knight. She broke her plum.

Reader 1:

It held by far the most expensive jewelry of all. The damsel once again made a bargain with the witch's daughter. The damsel gave the witch's daughter the jewelry from the plum for one more chance to sleep in the young knight's chamber.

Reader 2:

Once again the old washerwife took a sleeping drink to the young knight's chamber. He told her he couldn't drink it without sweetening.

Reader 1:

Away the old washerwife flew to get some honey to sweeten the knight's drink. While she was gone, the knight poured out the drink. He made the old washerwife think he had drunk it.

Reader 2:

The knight went to bed. The young woman began her watch. As before, she began singing, "Seven long years I served for thee. The glassy hill I climbed for thee. Thy bloody clothes I wrang for thee. Wilt thou not wake and turn to me?"

Reader 1:

This time the knight heard the damsel's song. She told him all about what had happened to her. He told her about defeating the Old One and regaining his human shape. He told her how long he had looked for her in the magic glen.

Reader 2:
The next day the old witch washerwife and her daughter were chased away. The knight and the damsel were married. Everyone says they are living happily together to this day.

Glossary

bannock   a kind of oatmeal or barley cake baked on a griddle

chamber   a bedroom or room in a house

coach-and-four   a four-wheeled carriage pulled by four horses

coach-and-six   a four-wheeled carriage pulled by six horses

collop   a small slice of meat

damsel   a young unmarried woman

glen   a small valley

grave   very serious

smith   one who shapes metals into simple tools by hammering

washerwife   a mature woman who washes clothes for others

weary   tired

The Brave Little Tailor

Story Introduction

In the "The Brave Little Tailor," an adaptation of a Brothers Grimm fairy tale, the little tailor kills seven flies with one stroke. This deed gives the tailor such self-confidence that he decides to take a trip and tell the whole world about his bravery.

Reader 1:

One summer morning a little tailor was sitting at his table by the window. He was very happy. He sewed with all his might. Just then a poor lady came down the street. She cried, "Good jams, cheap! Good jams, cheap!"

Reader 2:

The little tailor looked out the window. He said, "Come, dear woman. Here you will get rid of your goods. Unpack all your pots for me."

Reader 1:

He looked in each pot. He lifted them up. He put his nose in them.

Reader 2:

Finally he said, "The jam seems to be good. Weigh me out four ounces, dear woman."

Reader 1:

The woman had hoped for a much better sale. After she gave the tailor his four ounces, she went away angrily.

Reader 2:

"Now, this jam shall be blessed by God. It shall give me health and strength," said the tailor.

Reader 1:

He took bread from the cupboard. He cut across the loaf and spread jam over it so it would taste sweet.

Reader 2:

"I'll just finish sewing this jacket before I take a bite," thought the tailor. He laid the bread near him. He was very happy!

Reader 1:

He sewed on and on. In the meantime, the smell of the sweet jam rose to where flies were sitting in great numbers. They quickly flew to the pot of jam.

Reader 2:

"Who invited you? Shoo! Get away from here," shouted the tailor.

Reader 1:

The flies were hard to turn away. They kept coming back in greater numbers. Finally the little tailor lost his patience.

Reader 2:

He took a piece of cloth from under his work table. "I'll give it to you. I will hit you hard!"

Reader 1:

Swat! went the cloth. The tailor drew the cloth away. There lay before him seven dead flies.

Reader 2:

"Oh, how I admire my own bravery," thought the little tailor. "The whole town should know about this!"

Reader 1:

He quickly cut himself a girdle. He sewed the girdle and embroidered in large letters SEVEN AT ONE STROKE.

Reader 2:

The little tailor looked about him. He decided his workshop was too small for him. He decided to go on a trip and tell the whole world about his bravery. He looked about to see what he could take with him on his trip.

Reader 1:

He found only an old cheese. He put it in his pocket. Outside his door, he found a bird caught in a thicket. He put it in his pocket with the cheese. He took to the road boldly. The road led up a mountain. At the top sat a powerful giant, looking around peacefully.

Reader 2:

"Good day, sir, I like the way you are looking over the world. I am on my way to try my luck. Do you want to go with me?" asked the brave little tailor.

Reader 1:

"You ragamuffin! You miserable creature! Get out of my sight," stormed the giant.

Reader 2:

As he unbuttoned his coat, the little tailor said, "Let me just show you who I am! There, you may read what kind of man I am!"

Reader 1:

"Seven at one stroke!" read the giant. The giant thought the seven had been men. He was impressed! He had more respect for the tiny tailor. He decided he would test the tailor. He chose a stone. He squeezed it until water dropped out. "Let me see you do that," challenged the giant.

Reader 2:

"Is that all? Why that is child's play!" said the tailor. He put his hand in his pocket. He brought out the soft cheese. He pressed it. Water ran out of it.

Reader 1:

The giant did not know what to say. He picked up another stone. He threw it so high the eye could hardly see it. "Let me see you do that," bellowed the giant.

Reader 2:

"That's well thrown," said the tailor. "But the stone came down to earth again. I will throw one that will not come back at all."

Reader 1:

He put his hand in his pocket. He took out the bird and threw it into the air. The bird was happy to be free. It rose and flew away. It never came back.

Reader 2:

"How does that shot please you, sir?" asked the brave little tailor.

Reader 1:

"You certainly can throw. Now we'll see if you can carry anything properly," said the giant.

Reader 2:

The giant took the little tailor to a huge oak tree.

Reader 1:

"If you are strong enough, help me carry this felled tree out of the forest," said the giant.

Reader 2:

"Surely," agreed the little tailor. "You take the trunk on your shoulders. I will carry the branches and the twigs. They are the heaviest."

Reader 1:

The giant took the trunk on his shoulders. The tailor sat on a branch. The giant could not look around. He had to carry away the whole tree and the little tailor too.

Reader 2:

The tailor was happy. He sat and sang at the top of his voice. He acted as if carrying the tree were child's play.

Reader 1:

Finally the load was too much for the giant. "I must let the tree fall!"

Reader 2:

The tailor jumped down. He took hold of the tree with both arms. He looked as if he had been carrying it. "You are such a great fellow. Yet, you cannot even carry the tree!" he chided.

Reader 1:

They walked on together. They passed a cherry tree. The giant took hold of the top of the tree where the ripest fruit was. He put the branch in the tailor's hands.

From *Fairy Tales for Two Readers.* © 1995. Teacher Ideas Press. (800) 237-6124.

Reader 2:

The little tailor was too weak to hold the tree. When the giant let go, the limb sprang back. The tailor was tossed high into the air.

Reader 1:

"What is this? Do you not have the strength to hold a small twig?" asked the giant.

Reader 2:

"Oh, I have strength! Holding that twig is nothing for a man who struck down seven at one blow. I jumped over the tree!" bragged the brave little tailor.

Reader 1:

The giant tried to jump. He could not get over the tree. He fell flat upon the branches. As he picked himself up, he said, "Little man, if you are such a brave fellow, come spend the night in our cavern."

Reader 2:

The little tailor went with him into the cavern. Other giants were sitting around a fire. Each of them was eating a roasted lamb. The tailor looked all around. "This place is much bigger than my workshop," he thought.

Reader 1:

The giant showed the little tailor where he was to sleep. Since the bed was too big for the little tailor, he crept into a corner of the cave and slept.

Reader 2:

By midnight the giant thought the little tailor was asleep. He took a great, hot iron bar. He cut through the bed with one blow. He thought he had finished the tailor for good.

Reader 1:

At dawn the giants went into the forest. They had long forgotten the brave little tailor. Suddenly, up he walked.

Reader 2:

The giants were very scared! They were afraid the little tailor would strike them all dead. They quickly ran away.

Reader 1:

The little tailor walked on. Finally he came to the courtyard of a royal palace. He was weary, so he lay down on the grass and fell asleep.

Reader 2:

As he slept, the people gazed at him. They read the words embroidered on his girdle.

Reader 1:

"Seven at one stroke!" They were amazed. "What great warrior is this? He must be a mighty lord."

Reader 2:

They ran to tell the king about this mighty warrior.

Reader 1:

The king sent his couriers to ask the brave little tailor to join the army.

Reader 2:

"Why, that is the very reason I came here. I am ready to join the king's army!" said the brave little tailor.

Reader 1:

The soldiers were very upset. "What is to be the end of this?" they asked. "If we quarrel with him, seven of us may fall at every blow. Not one of us can stand against him! We are not prepared to stay with a man who kills seven at one stroke!"

Reader 2:

The king hated to lose all his faithful servants. At the same time, he hated to dismiss the tailor. He was afraid the tailor would kill all his people and place himself on the throne.

Reader 1:

Finally the king sent for the tailor. The king said to the tailor, "There are two giants living in a forest. They rob, murder, ravage and burn. No one can get near them. If you will kill those two giants, I will give you my daughter in marriage and half my kingdom. I will give you a hundred horsemen to help you."

Reader 2:

The tailor was amazed. He said, "That is a fine offer for a man like me. It's not every day I am offered a beautiful princess and half a kingdom. I can kill the giants! I don't need a hundred horsemen. If I can kill seven with one blow, I don't need to be afraid of two."

Reader 1:

The brave little tailor and the hundred horsemen went into the forest. The tailor told the horsemen to wait. He wanted to finish off the giants by himself.

Reader 2:

The tailor soon found the two giants sleeping under a tree. He grabbed a pocketful of rocks and climbed up a tree. He let a stone fall on the breast of one of the giants.

Reader 1:

For a long time the giant felt nothing. At last he awakened and asked the other giant, "Why are you hitting me?"

Reader 2:

"You must be dreaming. I am not hitting you," answered the other giant.

Reader 1:

They went to sleep again. The tailor threw another rock, hitting the second giant.

Reader 2:

"What is the meaning of this? Why are you pelting me?" he screamed.

Reader 1:

"I am not pelting you!" the first giant argued. They fussed and fussed at each other. Finally they closed their eyes once more.

Reader 2:

The little tailor began his game again. He picked out the biggest stone. He threw it as hard as he could at the breast of the first giant.

Reader 1:

"That's enough!" screamed the first giant. He sprang at the other giant. They tore up the trees and the ground as they fought. Finally they both fell down dead.

From *Fairy Tales for Two Readers.* © 1995. Teacher Ideas Press. (800) 237-6124.

Reader 2:

The tailor jumped down from his perch. "Gee, I am lucky they did not tear up the tree in which I was sitting."

Reader 1:

He drew his sword and thrust it into each of the giants. Then he went out to the horsemen.

Reader 2:

"The work is done," announced the brave little tailor. "I finished off the giants! It was hard work! They fought hard! It was really to no purpose, though. You remember I have killed seven with one blow."

Reader 1:

The horsemen could not believe their eyes. The tailor was not wounded. Not even one hair was out of place! They hurried to check out what the tailor said. Sure enough, there were the dead giants and the broken trees.

Reader 2:

The little tailor marched out of the forest. He hurried to see the king and demanded his reward.

Reader 1:

The king said, "There is just one more thing you need to do before you take my daughter and half my kingdom. There's a unicorn that roams the forest. You must catch it first."

Reader 2:

The tailor boasted, "I'm not afraid of a unicorn. One unicorn is less than two giants. Seven at one blow is my kind of affair!"

Reader 1:

The tailor took a rope and an axe with him into the forest. Again, he demanded the hundred horsemen wait outside. Soon he found the unicorn.

Reader 2:

As the unicorn rushed to gore him, the tailor said to himself, "Softly, softly, it cannot be done as quickly as that!"

Reader 1:

The tailor stood very still and waited. As the unicorn came close, the tailor jumped behind a tree.

Reader 2:

The unicorn charged into the tree. There his horn stuck so fast he could not pull away.

Reader 1:

The brave little tailor came from behind the tree. He put a rope around the unicorn's neck.

Reader 2:

He took his axe and cut the horn out of the tree. He led the unicorn away to the king, but the king still would not give him his promised reward.

Reader 1:

"Now you must catch the wild boar that causes great havoc in the forest," said the king.

Reader 2:

Once again the tailor went into the forest alone. The boar saw him and charged. Just as the boar was about to throw him to the ground, the tailor turned and ran into a nearby chapel.

Reader 1:

The boar ran after him. The tailor ran out of the chapel as the boar ran in. The tailor shut the door, and the boar was penned in the chapel.

Reader 2:

Once again the tailor went to collect his prizes.

Reader 1:

The wedding was held. A tailor became a king!

Reader 2:

Later the queen heard her husband say in his dreams, "Boy, make me a doublet. Patch the pantaloons. If you don't, I will rap you with my yardstick!"

From *Fairy Tales for Two Readers.* © 1995. Teacher Ideas Press. (800) 237-6124.

Reader 1:

The queen soon grew unhappy with her husband, the former tailor. Although the little tailor tried his best, he could not seem to make his wife happy.

Reader 2:

Her father tried to comfort his lovely daughter.

Reader 1:

Finally the old king told her, "Leave your bedroom door unlocked tonight. My servants will remove the tailor when he falls asleep."

Reader 2:

The armor-bearer liked the little tailor. He told the tailor of the old king's plans.

Reader 1:

The appointed hour came. The little tailor pretended to sleep.

Reader 2:

The tailor spoke while pretending to sleep, "Boy, make me a doublet. Patch the pantaloons. If you don't, I will rap you with my yardstick. I killed two giants. I brought away one unicorn. I caught a wild boar. I am not afraid of those who stand outside my room."

Reader 1:

The men outside the room vanished. They were happy to get away with their lives.

Reader 2:

The little tailor remained a king to the end of his life.

Glossary

armor-bearer   a person, usually a young boy, who carries the weapons of a warrior

cavern   a large cave

chapel   a place of worship smaller than a church

chide   to scold or blame

courier   a messenger

cupboard   a closet or cabinet with shelves

doublet   an outer garment with or without sleeves

embroidery   needlework that is ornamental

fell   to cut down

girdle   anything that encircles like a belt

gore   to wound with horns

havoc   general destruction, ruin

pantaloons   tight-fitting trousers and stockings

pelting   a beating

ragamuffin   a youngster who wears ragged clothes

ravage   to wreck, destroy

tailor   one who makes or repairs garments for men or women

thicket   a dense growth of shrubs or undergrowth

unicorn   a mythical horselike animal with one horn

warrior   a soldier

Cap O' Rushes

Story Introduction

In "Cap O' Rushes," a tale of magic adapted from one of Joseph Jacobs's English fairy tales, Cap O' Rushes not only wins the love of the master's son, but she also proves the depth of her love and respect for her own father, despite his initial misunderstanding of the meaning of her words.

Reader 1:
A very rich old gentleman decided he would find out how fond of him his three daughters were.

Reader 2:
"How much do you love me, my dear oldest daughter?" he asked.

Reader 1:
"Why, I love you as I love my life," she answered.

Reader 2:
"That's good. Now, my dear second daughter, how much do you love me?"

Reader 1:
"Why, I love you better than all the world."

Reader 2:
"That's good. And, my dear third daughter, how much do you love me?"

From *Fairy Tales for Two Readers.* © 1995. Teacher Ideas Press. (800) 237-6124.

Reader 1:

Now, the third and youngest daughter didn't think the question was fair. She knew she loved her father more than her sisters did. So she said, "I love you as much as fresh meat loves salt."

Reader 2:

The old gentleman became angry.

Reader 1:

He never should have asked that question.

Reader 2:

"That means you don't love me at all. You are ungrateful! You can no longer live in my house!"

Reader 1:

After that, there just didn't seem to be any way the youngest daughter could prove her love to her father. She decided to take her three dresses and go out into the wide world.

Reader 2:

On and on she went. Finally she came to a swamp. There she gathered a bunch of rushes from which she made a cloak. The cloak covered her from head to foot.

Reader 1:

She hid her three fine dresses under the dry roots of a tree by a brook and travelled on until she came to a great house. "Do you want a maid? I need work and a home. I don't have to have any wages," she said to the lady of the house.

Reader 2:

"Well, if you don't mind washing the pots and scraping the saucepans, you may stay," said the lady.

Reader 1:

The youngest daughter decided to stay. She washed the pots and scraped the pans. She did all the dirty work. Because she would not tell the people in the great house her name, they called her Cap O' Rushes.

Reader 2:

One day there was to be a great dance at the master's house. All the servants were allowed to go and watch.

Reader 1:

Cap O' Rushes said she was too tired to go and that she would stay home.

Reader 2:

When everyone was gone, she took off her cape of rushes and washed herself in the clear brook. Then she put on a beautiful silver dress and appeared at the ball.

Reader 1:

As soon as the master's son saw Cap O' Rushes, he fell in love with her. He would not dance with anyone else.

Reader 2:

Before the dance was over, Cap O' Rushes slipped away and hurried home.

Reader 1:

When the other maids came home, Cap O' Rushes was sound asleep.

Reader 2:

The next morning one of the maids said to Cap O' Rushes, "You did miss a sight. The prettiest lady you ever saw came to the ball. The young master never took his eyes off her."

Reader 1:

"Well, I wish I could have seen her," said Cap O' Rushes.

Reader 2:

"There's going to be another dance this evening. Maybe she will be there," suggested one of the maids.

Reader 1:

When the evening came, though, Cap O' Rushes was again too tired to go to the ball.

Reader 2:

Cap O' Rushes waited until everyone was out of the house. Again she washed herself in the brook. This time she put on a dress made of gold and then appeared at the ball.

Reader 1:

The master's son was waiting for her. He danced with no one else. He never took his eyes off her.

Reader 2:
Before the dance was over, Cap O' Rushes slipped away. She hurried home.

Reader 1:
When the maids came back, Cap O' Rushes pretended to be asleep with her cape of rushes.

Reader 2:
"Well, Cap O' Rushes, you should have been at the ball. The lady was there again, gay and gallant. The young master never took his eyes off her," said the servant.

Reader 1:
"Dear me," sighed Cap O' Rushes, "I would like to have seen her."

Reader 2:
"There's a dance again this evening. You must go with us. She's sure to be there," said another servant.

Reader 1:
When evening came, Cap O' Rushes said for the third time that she was too tired to go to the dance. The servants tried to persuade her to go, but she still refused.

Reader 2:
When they were all gone, she took off her cape of rushes and bathed in the brook.

Reader 1:
This time she put on a dress made out of the feathers of all the birds that fly in the air. Then she appeared at the dance.

Reader 2:
The master's son was very glad to see her. He danced only with her and never took his eyes off her.

Reader 1:
Cap O' Rushes would not tell the master's son her name. She also would not tell him where she lived.

Reader 2:
He gave her a ring and told her if he never saw her again, he would die.

Reader 1:

Cap O' Rushes slipped away before the dance was over. Home she went.

Reader 2:

When the maids arrived home, Cap O' Rushes pretended to be asleep.

Reader 1:

The next morning the maids could hardly wait to report to Cap O' Rushes.

Reader 2:

"Oh, Cap O' Rushes, you didn't come last night, and now you will never see the lady. There will be no more dances."

Reader 1:

The master's son tried very hard to find the lady he loved. But go where he might and ask whom he would, he never heard a thing about her. His health grew worse and worse because he could not find his love.

Reader 2:

At last the master's son was so ill he had to go to bed. He was going to die without his beautiful lady. The cook rushed to make some gruel for the young master.

Reader 1:

Just then Cap O' Rushes came to the master's house. "What are you doing?" she asked the cook.

Reader 2:

"I'm going to make some gruel for the young master. It seems he's dying for love of the lady," answered the cook.

Reader 1:

Cap O' Rushes insisted that she be allowed to make the gruel. At first the cook would not let her, but she finally agreed to let Cap O' Rushes make the gruel.

Reader 2:

Cap O' Rushes made the gruel and slipped her ring into it. The cook took the gruel upstairs to the master's son.

Reader 1:

The young man drank the gruel, then he saw the ring in the bottom of the bowl.

Reader 2:

He demanded, "Send for the cook! I must know who made this gruel!"

Reader 1:

"I did!" said the cook.

Reader 2:

"No, you did not. Say who did, and you will not be harmed," demanded the master's son.

Reader 1:

"Well, then, it was Cap O' Rushes," said the cook.

Reader 2:

"Come here, Cap O' Rushes. Did you make the gruel?" asked the master's son.

Reader 1:

"Yes, I did," said Cap O' Rushes.

Reader 2:

"Where did you get this ring?" he asked.

Reader 1:

"From him that gave it to me," answered Cap O' Rushes.

Reader 2:

"Who are you, then?" asked the master's son.

Reader 1:

"I'll show you," said Cap O' Rushes.

Reader 2:

She pulled off her cape of rushes. There she was in her beautiful clothes. Her lovely hair was hanging down to her waist.

Reader 1:

The master's son soon got well. Everyone far and near was invited to the wedding.

Reader 2:

The father of Cap O' Rushes was invited. No one knew he was the father of the bride because Cap O' Rushes would not tell anyone who she really was.

Reader 1:

Before the wedding, Cap O' Rushes went to the cook and said, "I want you to prepare every dish of meat without putting a mite o' salt in it."

Reader 2:

"That will taste nasty!" replied the cook.

Reader 1:

"Never mind that," said Cap O' Rushes.

Reader 2:

The wedding day came. Cap O' Rushes and the master's son were married. After the wedding, the grand company sat down to the wedding feast.

Reader 1:

When they began to eat the meat, it was tasteless. No one could eat it.

Reader 2:

Cap O' Rushes watched her father carefully as he tried one dish after another. Finally he burst out crying.

Reader 1:

Everyone wanted to know why he was crying.

Reader 2:

He said, "I once had a daughter. I asked her how much she loved me. She said, 'As much as fresh meat loves salt.' I turned her away from my door because I thought she meant she did not love me. Now I see that she meant that she loved me best of all. To think, she may be dead now for all I know."

Reader 1:

Cap O' Rushes got up from her place. She ran to her father and threw her arms around his neck. "No, Father, here I am! I am your daughter."

Reader 2:

They all lived happily ever after.

Glossary

cape a sleeveless garment that hangs loosely about the shoulders

cloak a loose garment, often hooded, that usually has no sleeves

gruel food made by boiling grain in water or milk, something like watery oatmeal or Cream of Wheat

mite a small amount

rushes tall grasses that grow in a marsh

Chicken Little

Story Introduction

"Chicken Little" is an adaptation of one of Joseph Jacobs's English fairy tales. When a nut hits Chicken Little on the tail, she decides the sky is falling. As she runs to tell the king, she also alarms the friends she meets along the way. Finally, Turkey Lurkey teaches Chicken Little a lesson: One must not jump to conclusions too quickly.

Reader 1:

One sunny, summer day Chicken Little ran into her garden. She looked for something to eat.

Reader 2:

She looked under a big tree. Whack! Something hit her on the tail.

Reader 1:

"Oh, oh, that hurt," chirped Chicken Little. "Is the sky falling? Oh, no, maybe the sky is falling! I must run to tell the king!"

Reader 2:

Away went Chicken Little to tell the king. She ran and ran and ran. Soon she met Henny Penny.

Reader 1:

"Oh, Henny Penny, the sky is falling! The sky is falling!"

Reader 2:

"How do you know?" asked Henny Penny, as she jogged along with Chicken Little.

Reader 1:

"With my big, chicken eyes, I saw it. With my big, chicken ears, I heard it. A piece of it whacked me on my tail. I must go tell the king."

Reader 2:

"Wait, I will go with you!" said Henny Penny.

Reader 1:

Chicken Little and Henny Penny ran to tell the king.

Reader 2:

They ran and ran. Soon they met Cocky Locky.

Reader 1:

"Good morning, Cocky Locky, did you know the sky is falling?" cried Chicken Little.

Reader 2:

"The sky is falling? How do you know the sky is falling?" asked Cocky Locky.

Reader 1:

"With my big, chicken eyes, I saw it. With my big, chicken ears, I heard it. A piece of it whacked me on my tail! We are going to tell the king!" said Chicken Little.

Reader 2:

"Let me go with you!" said Cocky Locky.

Reader 1:

So Chicken Little, Henny Penny, and Cocky Locky ran to tell the king.

Reader 2:

They ran and ran. Soon they met Goosey Poosey.

Reader 1:

"Good morning, Goosey Poosey, did you know the sky is falling?" cried Chicken Little.

Reader 2:

"The sky is falling? How do you know?" asked Goosey Poosey.

Reader 1:

"With my big, chicken eyes, I saw it. With my big, chicken ears, I heard it. A piece of it whacked me on my tail! We are going to tell the king!" said Chicken Little.

Reader 2:

"Let me go, too!" said Goosey Poosey.

Reader 1:

So Chicken Little, Henny Penny, Cocky Locky, and Goosey Poosey ran to tell the king.

Reader 2:

They ran and ran. They met Turkey Lurkey. "Where are you going?" asked Turkey Lurkey.

Reader 1:

"Oh, my friend, Turkey Lurkey! The sky is falling! The sky is falling!" cried Chicken Little.

Reader 2:

"Who told you the sky is falling? That is not true!" said Turkey Lurkey.

Reader 1:

"With my big, chicken eyes, I saw it. With my big, chicken ears, I heard it. A piece of it whacked me on my tail! We are going to tell the king!" said Chicken Little.

Reader 2:

Turkey Lurkey said slowly, "No, Chicken Little, let's not go see the king yet. Let's go back to the garden. First we must see what fell on your tail!" said Turkey Lurkey.

Reader 1:

"I do not have time to go to the garden! I know the sky is falling!" said Chicken Little.

Reader 2:

"All of you come with me! Come with me this very minute!" demanded Turkey Lurkey.

Reader 1:

Then Turkey Lurkey, Goosey Poosey, Cocky Locky, and Henny Penny ran and ran and ran.

Reader 2:

Chicken Little ran and ran and ran. They all ran back to the garden.

Reader 1:

Turkey Lurkey looked at the sky. They all looked up at the sky.

Reader 2:

Turkey Lurkey looked and looked under the big tree. Suddenly he saw something!

Reader 1:

He saw a nut under the tree. Goosey Poosey, Cocky Locky, Henny Penny, and Chicken Little saw the nut!

Reader 2:

"Do you think this nut might have hit you, Chicken Little?" asked Turkey Lurkey.

Reader 1:

"Yes, Chicken Little, you must be mistaken," said Goosey Poosey, Cocky Locky, and Henny Penny.

Reader 2:

"Look carefully, Chicken Little," said Turkey Lurkey. "The sky is not really falling."

Reader 1:

"A nut fell on your tail, a nut fell on your tail," sang Goosey Poosey, Cocky Locky, and Henny Penny. "Chicken Little, you must learn to look before you prattle!"

Glossary

cock rooster

prattle to talk foolishly

From *Fairy Tales for Two Readers.* © 1995. Teacher Ideas Press. (800) 237-6124.

Clever Elsie

Story Introduction

"Clever Elsie," adapted from a Brothers Grimm fairy tale, is laced with jokes and anecdotes. Elsie's parents think she is very smart, but she must prove her cleverness to Hans, her admirer.

Reader 1:

Years ago in Germany, a man and his wife had a daughter they called Clever Elsie because they thought she was the smartest young woman in the land.

Reader 2:

One day her father said, "We will get her married!"

Reader 1:

Her mother said, "Oh, if someone, anyone would have her!"

Reader 2:

At last, a man named Hans came to woo Elsie.

Reader 1:

Hans said the one thing he wanted was a smart wife.

Reader 2:

"Oh, Elsie is very smart," said her father.

Reader 1:

"Why, she can see the wind coming up the street! She can hear flies coughing," agreed her mother.

Reader 2:

"Well, if she is not really smart, I will not have her," said Hans.

Reader 1:

At dinner the mother said, "Elsie, go to the cellar and get something to drink!"

Reader 2:

Clever Elsie took the pitcher from the wall. She went into the cellar. She found a chair. She sat in front of the barrel.

Reader 1:

She put the pitcher under the barrel and turned the tap. The drink ran into the pitcher.

Reader 2:

Elsie looked all around. She looked up at the wall. Just above her head, Elsie saw a pick-axe.

Reader 1:

Clever Elsie began to weep and to blubber. "If I get Hans, we may have a child. He will grow big. We will send him to the cellar to get the drink. The pick-axe may fall on his head and kill him."

Reader 2:

Elsie sat down and cried. She cried over the misfortune that lay before her. The people upstairs waited for their drink, but Elsie did not come.

Reader 1:

Elsie's mother sent the maid to the cellar. "See where Elsie is!"

Reader 2:

The maid found Elsie sitting in front of the barrel, sobbing loudly. The maid asked, "Elsie, why do you weep?"

Reader 1:

"If I get Hans, we may have a child. He will grow big. We will send him to the cellar to get the drink. The pick-axe may fall on his head and kill him," cried Elsie.

Reader 2:

"What a clever Elsie we have!" said the maid. The maid sat down beside Elsie. Together they wept loudly over Elsie's misfortune.

Reader 1:

The people upstairs waited for their drink, but the maid did not come back.

Reader 2:

Elsie's father said to the hired boy, "Go down into the cellar. See where Elsie and the maid are."

Reader 1:

The boy went down into the cellar. There sat Clever Elsie and the maid crying together.

Reader 2:

"Why are you crying?" asked the boy.

Reader 1:

"If I get Hans, we may have a child. He will grow big. We will send him to the cellar to get the drink. The pick-axe may fall on his head and kill him," cried Elsie.

Reader 2:

"What a clever Elsie we have!" said the hired boy. The boy sat down by Elsie's side. Elsie, the maid, and the hired boy cried loudly.

Reader 1:

The people upstairs waited, but the boy did not return.

Reader 2:

Finally the father said to Elsie's mother, "Go down in the cellar. See where Elsie is."

Reader 1:

The mother went into the cellar. There sat Elsie, the maid, and the hired boy, crying together. "What's the matter here?" asked the mother.

Reader 2:

Elsie, the maid, and the hired boy looked sadly at the mother and cried even louder.

Reader 1:

Finally Elsie blubbered, "If I get Hans, we may have a child. He will grow big. We will send him to the cellar to get the drink. The pick-axe may fall on his head and kill him."

Reader 2:

The mother blinked her eyes in amazement. She thought her daughter was so clever.

Reader 1:

"What a clever Elsie we have!" said her mother. The mother sat down by the hired boy. They all wept loudly.

Reader 2:

The father waited upstairs. Finally he said, "I must go into the cellar. I must see where Elsie is!"

Reader 1:

There sat Elsie, the maid, the hired boy, and the mother crying.

Reader 2:

"What's wrong here?" asked Elsie's father.

Reader 1:

"If I marry Hans, we may have a child. He will grow big. We will send him to the cellar to get the drink. The pick-axe may fall on his head and kill him," cried Elsie.

Reader 2:

"Oh, what a clever, clever Elsie!" said her father.

Reader 1:

Hans stayed upstairs alone for a long time. Finally he decided to go into the cellar.

Reader 2:

Hans found the five of them sitting and crying. Each one was sobbing more loudly than the other. "What is the matter?" asked Hans.

Reader 1:

"If we marry, dear Hans, we may have a child. He will grow big," blubbered Elsie. "We will send him to the cellar to get the drink. The pick-axe may fall on his head and kill him."

Reader 2:

"What a clever Elsie we have here!" said Hans. He took Elsie's hand, led her upstairs, and married her.

Reader 1:

They were married for a long time.

Reader 2:

One day Hans announced, "Wife, I am going to work. I will earn money for us. You go cut the corn so we can have some bread."

Reader 1:

"Yes, dear Hans, I will do that," said Elsie.

Reader 2:

Hans left. Elsie cooked some broth to take to the field.

Reader 1:

Just as she came to the field, she started talking to herself. "What shall I do? Shall I cut first? Or, shall I eat first? Oh, I will eat first."

Reader 2:

She drank her cup of broth. Then she spoke to herself again.

Reader 1:

"What shall I do? Shall I cut first? Or, shall I sleep first? I will sleep first." She lay down in the corn and fell asleep.

Reader 2:

Hans came home. He waited a long time for Elsie. She did not come. "What a clever Elsie I have! She works so hard she doesn't even come home to eat," said Hans.

Reader 1:

Evening came. Elsie still was not home. Hans went to see how much corn Elsie had cut.

Reader 2:

Nothing was cut. Elsie was lying down. She had fallen asleep in the corn.

Reader 1:

Hans decided to play a joke on Elsie. He hurried home and got a fowler's net. He put little bells around the net.

Reader 2:

He ran back to the field and put the fowler's net over Clever Elsie. Elsie went on sleeping.

Reader 1:

Hans ran home, shut the door to his house, sat in his chair, and worked.

Reader 2:

When it was very dark, Clever Elsie awakened. She got up.

Reader 1:

There was jingling all around her. The bells rang with each step Elsie took.

Reader 2:

She was so scared she couldn't decide whether she really was Clever Elsie or not.

Reader 1:

"Is it I, or is it not I?" she cried.

Reader 2:

She couldn't decide what the answer ought to be.

Reader 1:

Finally she thought, "I will go home and ask if it be not I. Surely Hans will know!"

Reader 2:

Elsie ran home. The door was shut!

Reader 1:

She knocked at the window and cried. "Hans, is Elsie within?"

Reader 2:

"Yes, she is within," said Hans.

Reader 1:

"Ah, heavens, then it is not I!" Elsie cried.

Reader 2:

Elsie ran to another house. The people inside heard the jingling of bells. They would not open the door. She could not get anyone to open the door for her.

Reader 1:

Storytellers say Elsie ran out of the village, and no one has seen her since.

Glossary

anecdote   a short story about an interesting or funny event

barrel   a large container that is usually made of wood or metal

blubber   to cry noisily

cellar   a room that is wholly or partly underground

fowler   one who cares for chickens

pick-axe   an axe that has a pointed pick on one end

woo   to seek someone's love or affection

The Cunning
Little Tailor

Story Introduction

Three tailors try to win the love of a princess. One of them, the smallest and least successful, proves to be the most resourceful. He solves the princess's riddle and eventually wins her hand in marriage in this story adapted from a Brothers Grimm fairy tale.

Reader 1:

Once upon a time there was a princess who was very proud. She didn't want to marry.

Reader 2:

If a suitor called, she always gave him a riddle to solve.

Reader 1:

She said that whoever solved her riddle could marry her, but no one had been able to figure out the answer.

Reader 2:

Three tailors decided to try their luck at solving the riddle.

Reader 1:

Two of the tailors thought there was no job too difficult for them. Each was sure he would win the princess.

Reader 2:

The third tailor, a small man, was harum-scarum and reckless. He was not a very good tailor. In fact, he had never found anything at which he was really good.

Reader 1:

The little tailor decided the princess's offer was the very thing he needed to change his luck.

Reader 2:

The other two tailors told the little tailor to just stay home. They thought he didn't know enough to win the princess's hand in marriage.

Reader 1:

The little tailor was not discouraged. He set to work planning at once. Then he went forth as if the whole world were his.

Reader 2:

The three tailors presented themselves to the princess.

Reader 1:

She wondered, "Is it possible that the right man has come?"

Reader 2:

She was ready to give her riddle to the tailors.

Reader 1:

"I have two different colors of hair on my head. What are the colors of my hair?" asked the princess.

Reader 2:

The first tailor said, "If that be all, it must be black and white. It is like the cloth that is called pepper and salt."

Reader 1:

"Wrongly guessed!" said the princess.

Reader 2:

"Well, if it's not black and white," said the second tailor, "it is brown and red. It is like my father's Sunday coat."

Reader 1:

"Wrongly guessed," said the princess. "Let the third tailor give his answer! I can see he knows the answer for certain!" said the princess mockingly.

From *Fairy Tales for Two Readers*. © 1995. Teacher Ideas Press. (800) 237-6124.

Reader 2:

The third little tailor stepped forward. He said, "The princess has a silver and a golden hair on her head. Those are the two different colors!"

Reader 1:

When the princess heard this, she turned pale. She did not really want to marry the little tailor or any other man. But the third little tailor had solved her riddle!

Reader 2:

She had firmly believed no man on earth could ever guess her riddle.

Reader 1:

"You have not won me yet," said the princess. "There is something else you must do. Below, in the stable, is a bear. You must spend the night with the bear. If you are still alive in the morning, you may marry me."

Reader 2:

The bear would get rid of the tailor! He had eaten everyone who had ever fallen into his den.

Reader 1:

The little tailor was not afraid.

Reader 2:

"Boldly ventured is half won!" he said.

Reader 1:

Night came! The little tailor was led down to the bear's den. The growling bear was just about to set upon the little tailor!

Reader 2:

"Softly, softly, I will soon make you quiet," said the little tailor. He took some nuts from his pocket, cracked them, and ate the kernels.

Reader 1:

The bear watched closely. The nuts looked delicious. "Give me some of those nuts," he demanded.

Reader 2:

The tailor felt in his pockets. He brought out a handful of pebbles.

Reader 1:

The bear popped the pebbles in his mouth. "Ugh! What a stupid blockhead I am. I cannot even crack a nut! Here, little tailor, crack the nuts for me."

Reader 2:

"You have such a great mouth. You should be able to crack a small nut," said the tailor. "You see, I will take a nut like this in my mouth and crack it in two."

Reader 1:

"I must try again. If I watch you, I think I can do it," said the bear.

Reader 2:

The tailor again gave him a pebble. The bear tried and tried to crack it, but he was not able. He cracked his sharp teeth instead.

Reader 1:

When that was over, the tailor took out a violin from beneath his coat. He played soft music.

Reader 2:

When the bear heard the music, he began to dance. He danced and danced. The music pleased him so much.

Reader 1:

"Listen, is it difficult to fiddle?" asked the bear.

Reader 2:

"Easy enough for a child," said the little tailor. "Look, with the left hand, I lay my fingers on it. With the right, I stroke it with the bow. Out comes beautiful music."

Reader 1:

"Fiddling is a thing I should like to learn! Then I could dance whenever I felt like it. What do you think of that? Will you give me lessons?" asked the bear.

Reader 2:

"Of course," said the little tailor. "You may have a talent for it. Just let me see your claws. They are terribly long. I must cut your nails a little."

Reader 1:

The vise was brought. The bear put his paws on it. The little tailor screwed the vise tight enough to hold the bear.

Reader 2:

"Now, wait until I come with the scissors!" said the little tailor.

Reader 1:

He used the scissors to cut off the bear's claws. Then he left the growling bear trapped in the vise.

Reader 2:

The little tailor lay down in the corner of the stable on a bundle of straw. Quickly he fell asleep.

Reader 1:

The princess heard the bear growling fiercely during the night. She believed he was growling for joy—that he had put an end to the tailor.

Reader 2:

In the morning she arose carefree and happy. She peeked into the stable. The tailor stood gaily before her, healthy as a fish in water!

Reader 1:

The princess couldn't say another word against the wedding. She had given a promise to everyone.

Reader 2:

The king ordered a carriage. The princess was to drive to church with the tailor to be married.

Reader 1:

The two other tailors were jealous. They wanted to marry the princess. They went into the stable and let the bear out of the vise.

Reader 2:

The bear ran after the carriage in a great fury.

Reader 1:

The princess heard the bear snorting and growling. She was so afraid she began to cry. "The bear is behind us. He wants to get you!" cried the princess.

Reader 2:

The tailor was quick. He cried, "Do you remember the vise? Be off or you shall be put into it again."

Reader 1:

The bear heard the tailor. He turned around and ran away.

Reader 2:

The tailor drove quietly to church. The princess was married to him at once.

Reader 1:

Ever after they lived as happily as lovebirds.

Glossary

cunning   crafty or shrewd

harum-scarum   reckless; wild

kernel   the part of a nut that can be eaten

stable   a building that is set apart from a house and used for lodging and feeding horses or cattle

suitor   a man who dates a woman in hopes of marrying her

tailor   one who makes or repairs garments for men or women

venture   to risk

vise   a device that has two jaws which close with a lever or screw to hold objects

---

The Goose Girl

Story Introduction

A false maid-in-waiting wears royal apparel and prepares to marry the prince, while the real princess wears rags and herds the geese. The real princess keeps her vow to tell no one about this injustice, although she does tell a stove her secret! As in all fairy tales, including this adaptation from a Brothers Grimm fairy tale, the real princess is discovered in time to claim her prince in marriage, and everyone is served their just desserts.

Reader 1:

Once upon a time there was an old queen whose husband had been dead for many years.

Reader 2:

The queen had a beautiful daughter whom she loved very much.

Reader 1:

The time came for the princess to be married to a prince who lived far away.

Reader 2:

The old queen packed up the royal dowry for her daughter. There were chests full of silver and gold, precious jewels, and rich trinkets.

Reader 1:

The queen also gave the princess Falada, the horse who could speak.

Reader 2:

The queen demanded that her maid-in-waiting ride with the princess to the palace of the bridegroom prince.

Reader 1:

The sad hour of parting finally came.

Reader 2:

The old queen went to her bedroom. She took a small knife and cut her finger until it bled.

Reader 1:

She let three drops of blood fall on a white handkerchief. Then she gave the handkerchief to the princess.

Reader 2:

"Dear child, preserve this carefully. It will be of service to you on your way," said the queen.

Reader 1:

The princess tucked the handkerchief into her dress. She mounted Falada and rode away to meet her bridegroom.

Reader 2:

After she had ridden for a while, the princess became very thirsty.

Reader 1:

"I need a drink of water," said the princess to the maid-in-waiting. "Dismount and get me some water from the stream. Use the cup you brought for me."

Reader 2:

"If you're so thirsty, get off your horse yourself. Lie down and drink out of the stream. I don't choose to be your maid!" said the maid-in-waiting.

Reader 1:

The princess got down from Falada. She bent down over the water and drank.

Reader 2:

The maid-in-waiting would not let her drink out of the golden cup.

Reader 1:

"Ah, heavens!" sighed the princess.

Reader 2:

The three drops of blood whispered, "If your mother knew this, her heart would break in two."

Reader 1:
The princess was so humble she said nothing. She mounted her horse again.

Reader 2:
The princess rode miles further. Because the day was so hot and the sun so scorching, she became thirsty again. Finally they came to another stream.

Reader 1:
The princess cried out to the maid-in-waiting, "Dismount and give me some water in my golden cup!"

Reader 2:
"If you want a drink, get it yourself. I don't choose to be your maid," snorted the maid-in-waiting.

Reader 1:
In her great thirst, the queen's daughter got down from Falada. She bent over the flowing stream and wept. "Ah, heavens!" she sighed.

Reader 2:
The three drops of blood whispered, "If your mother knew this, her heart would break in two."

Reader 1:
As the princess was drinking, the handkerchief with the three drops of blood fell out of her dress. The water carried it away, and the princess lost the protection her mother had given her.

Reader 2:
The princess was so troubled she didn't even see the handkerchief float away. But, the maid-in-waiting had seen it!

Reader 1:
Now the maid-in-waiting knew she had full power over the princess.

Reader 2:
The princess started to remount Falada.

Reader 1:
The maid-in-waiting spoke crossly to her.

Reader 2:

"Falada is more suitable for me. My nag will do for you," she said.

Reader 1:

The princess was forced to be content with the maid-in-waiting's nag.

Reader 2:

Then the maid-in-waiting forced the princess to exchange her royal apparel for the maid's shabby clothes.

Reader 1:

Then the wicked maid-in-waiting forced the princess to swear to the clear sky above her that she would not say one word about the maid's deeds to anyone at the royal court.

Reader 2:

The maid promised that she would kill the princess if she so much as uttered a word!

Reader 1:

Falada saw and heard all this. She observed it well.

Reader 2:

The maid-in-waiting mounted Falada. The princess, who was the true bride, mounted the nag. They travelled onward until they entered the royal palace.

Reader 1:

There was great rejoicing. The prince ran to meet them. He lifted the maid-in-waiting from her horse. The false bride was carried upstairs. The real princess was left standing below.

Reader 2:

The old king looked out his window and saw the real princess standing in the courtyard. He noticed how delicate and beautiful she was.

Reader 1:

The old king went instantly to the royal apartment. He asked the false bride about the girl standing down below in the courtyard.

Reader 2:

"On my way here, I picked her up as a companion. Give her work so she won't stand idle," said the maid-in-waiting.

Reader 1:

"I don't have any work for her! Conrad, the little hired boy, tends the geese. Perhaps she could help him," said the king.

Reader 2:

Soon the false bride had an idea. She turned to the prince and said, "I beg you to do me a favor."

Reader 1:

"I will do so most willingly," said the young prince.

Reader 2:

"Send for a servant and have him get my horse out of my sight. Give her away! Stake her out! Get rid of her! She vexed me on my way here," demanded the maid-in-waiting.

Reader 1:

The truth was, she was afraid the horse might tell what had been done to the real princess.

Reader 2:

The real princess heard the news that Falada would be removed from the court. She secretly promised to pay the servant a piece of gold if he would perform a small service for her.

Reader 1:

"There is a great, dark gateway in the town which I must pass through with the geese. Would you be so good as to stake Falada out near it? That way I will be able to see that beautiful horse," said the princess.

Reader 2:

The servant promised to do just that. He staked Falada out beneath the dark gateway.

Reader 1:

Early in the morning, when she and Conrad drove their flock beneath the gateway, the princess said in passing, "Alas, Falada, standing there!"

Reader 2:

The horse answered, "Alas, young Queen, how ill you fare! If this your mother knew, her heart would break in two."

Reader 1:
Conrad and the princess went further out of town. They drove their geese out into the country.

Reader 2:
When they came to a meadow, the princess sat down and unbound her hair, which was like pure gold. Conrad couldn't believe his eyes. He was delighted by its brightness. He wanted to pluck out a few hairs.

Reader 1:
Then the princess sang: "Blow, blow thou gentle wind. Blow Conrad's little hat away. Make him chase it here and there, till I have braided all my hair."

Reader 2:
There came such a gust of wind that it blew Conrad's hat far away, across the countryside. He was forced to run after it.

Reader 1:
When Conrad came back, the princess had finished combing her hair and was putting it up again. He could not get even one hair.

Reader 2:
Conrad was so angry that he wouldn't speak to the princess. They sat silently watching the geese until evening. Then they went home.

Reader 1:
The next day when they were driving the geese out through the dark gateway, the real princess said, "Alas, Falada, standing there!"

Reader 2:
"Alas, young Queen, how ill you fare! If this your mother knew, her heart would break in two," replied the horse.

Reader 1:
The princess sat down again in the field and began to comb out her hair.

Reader 2:
Conrad was fascinated by its beauty. He ran and tried to clutch it.

Reader 1:

The princess said in haste, "Blow, blow thou gentle wind. Blow Conrad's little hat away. Make him chase it here and there, till I have braided all my hair."

Reader 2:

The wind blew Conrad's little hat right off his head, and he was forced to run after it.

Reader 1:

When he came back, the princess had her hair up. He could not get even one strand. There was nothing else to do but look after the geese until evening came.

Reader 2:

That evening, after they got home, Conrad went to see the king. "I won't tend the geese with that girl any longer!" he said.

Reader 1:

"Why not?" asked the king.

Reader 2:

"Oh, because she makes me angry the whole day long," admitted Conrad.

Reader 1:

"Well, for goodness' sake, what does she do to you?" asked the king.

Reader 2:

"In the morning, when we pass beneath the dark gateway with the flock, there is a horse standing near the gate, and she says to it, 'Alas, Falada, standing there!' And the horse replies, 'Alas, young Queen, how ill you fare! If this your mother knew, her heart would break in two.' "

Reader 1:

Conrad also told the king about the wind blowing his hat away.

Reader 2:

The old king told Conrad to drive his flock out again the next day.

Reader 1:

When morning came, the king hid behind the dark gateway. He heard the maiden speak to Falada.

Reader 2:

The king followed them into the country. He hid himself in the thicket in the meadow. Soon he saw with his own eyes the goose girl and the goose boy with their flock.

Reader 1:

He saw the girl sit down to plait her hair, which shone with radiance. He heard her say, "Blow, blow thou gentle wind. Blow Conrad's little hat away. Make him chase it here and there, till I have braided all my hair."

Reader 2:

A blast of wind came and carried off Conrad's hat. Conrad ran away after his hat while the maiden quietly went on combing and plaiting her hair.

Reader 1:

Quietly the old king slipped away and went home.

Reader 2:

When the goose girl came home that evening, the old king called her aside and asked why she did all these things.

Reader 1:

"I cannot tell you. I will not speak of my sorrows to any human being, for I have sworn not to do so by the heaven which is above me. If I tell you why I do these things, I will lose my life," she answered.

Reader 2:

The king suggested that she tell her sorrows to the iron stove.

Reader 1:

When the king went away, the real princess crept into the iron stove.

Reader 2:

She began to weep and lament. She emptied her whole heart.

Reader 1:

"Here am I, deserted by the whole world, and yet I am a king's daughter. A false maid-in-waiting has forced all this upon me. She has on my royal apparel. I have on her rags. She has taken my place with my bridegroom. I must perform menial service as a goose girl. If my mother knew this, her heart would break in two!"

From *Fairy Tales for Two Readers*. © 1995. Teacher Ideas Press. (800) 237-6124.

Reader 2:

The old king was standing outside by the stovepipe. He heard what the princess said. He went back inside and asked her to come out of the stove.

Reader 1:

He placed royal garments on her. She was beautiful!

Reader 2:

The old king called for his son. He explained that they had been lied to by the false bride, who was really only a maid-in-waiting. The goose girl standing before them was really the true bride.

Reader 1:

The prince rejoiced with all his heart when he saw his bride's beauty and youth. A great feast was prepared and all their good friends were invited.

Reader 2:

At the head of the table sat the bridegroom with the king's daughter on one hand and the wicked maid-in-waiting on the other.

Reader 1:

The maid-in-waiting did not recognize the princess in her dazzling array.

Reader 2:

When all had eaten and drunk and were merry, the old king asked the maid-in-waiting a riddle.

Reader 1:

"What punishment would a person deserve who had behaved in such and such a way?" The king recounted the whole story of what the maid-in-waiting had done to the princess.

Reader 2:

"She deserves no better fate than to be stripped entirely naked and put in a barrel which is studded inside with pointed nails. Two white horses should be harnessed to it. They should drag her along through one street after another," answered the maid-in-waiting, who was very wicked and cruel.

Reader 1:

"You have pronounced your own sentence. It shall be done unto you," announced the king.

Reader 2:
When the sentence had been carried out, the prince married his true bride. Together they reigned over their kingdom in peace and happiness.

Glossary

apparel   outer clothing

array   fine clothing

barrel   a large container that is usually made of wood or metal

clutch   to grab and hold tightly

dismount   to get off a horse

dowry   the money or property a wife brings to her marriage

humble   modest, free from pride

lament   to express sorrow

maid-in-waiting   a young woman in a queen's or princess's household appointed to wait upon or attend her

menial   lowly work often done by servants

mount   a horse

nag   an old worthless horse

plait   to braid hair

reign   to hold and exercise royal power

scorching   burning

strand   a single hair

thicket   thick, dense underbrush

trinkets   jewelry, a small ornament

vex   to provoke anger

Kate
Crackernuts

Story Introduction

The story of "Kate Crackernuts," adapted from one of Joseph Jacobs's English fairy tales, centers around Kate, her mother, and her step-sister Anne. Kate, the heroine, restores Anne's beauty, heals the sick prince, and finally marries him in this tale of good overcoming evil.

Reader 1:

The king and his first wife had a daughter named Anne.

Reader 2:

The king's second wife, the queen, had a daughter named Kate.

Reader 1:

Even though Anne was prettier than Kate, Kate was not jealous of her.

Reader 2:

The queen, however, was very jealous of Anne.

Reader 1:

Because she wanted to find a spell to spoil Anne's beauty, the queen visited the henwife, who was really a witch, to see what she would suggest.

Reader 2:

The henwife told the queen to have Anne fast, and then send the girl to see her the next morning.

Reader 1:

Early the next morning, before breakfast, the queen sent Anne to the henwife's house in the glen to get some fresh eggs.

Reader 2:

Anne picked up a basket for the eggs. As she passed through the kitchen, she picked up a crust of bread to eat along the way.

Reader 1:

Anne arrived at the henwife's house and asked for the eggs.

Reader 2:

The henwife told Anne to lift the lid off a crock.

Reader 1:

Anne lifted the lid, but nothing happened.

Reader 2:

The henwife said to Anne, "Go home to your mammie and tell her to keep her larder door locked."

Reader 1:

Anne went home and told the queen what the henwife had said.

Reader 2:

Then the queen knew Anne had eaten.

Reader 1:

The next morning the queen watched closely to make certain that Anne was fasting when she went to the henwife's house.

Reader 2:

Along the roadside the princess saw some country folk picking peas.

Reader 1:

Anne stopped and passed the time of day with them. As they talked together, she took a couple of pods and ate the peas.

Reader 2:

Finally Anne arrived at the henwife's house and asked for the eggs.

Reader 1:

The henwife told Anne to lift the lid off the crock.

Reader 2:

Anne lifted the lid, but nothing happened. The henwife grew very angry. She screamed, "Tell your mammie the pot won't boil if there's no fire under it."

Reader 1:

Anne went home and told the queen what the henwife had said.

Reader 2:

The third day the queen went with Anne to the henwife's house, and she made sure that Anne ate nothing. When Anne lifted the lid off the crock, her pretty head fell off. On jumped a sheep's head.

Reader 1:

Now the jealous queen was satisfied. Anne was no longer the prettiest.

Reader 2:

When Kate saw what had happened, she was sorry for Anne. She took a piece of white linen and wrapped it around her sister's head.

Reader 1:

Away the two went, hand in hand, to seek their fortunes together. Finally they came to a castle. Kate knocked on the door and asked to spend the night.

Reader 2:

They were invited into the castle of a king who had two sons. One of the sons was very ill. No one knew what was wrong with the boy.

Reader 1:

No one could sit beside his bed for a night. Those who tried were never seen again.

Reader 2:

The king offered a peck of silver to anyone who could live to tell the story of having spent the night beside his son's bed.

Reader 1:

Kate was a very brave girl. She offered to sit out the night by the prince's bedside.

Reader 2:

Nothing happened until midnight. As the twelve strokes rang from the clock in the castle tower, the sick prince got out of his bed. He dressed himself and slipped downstairs.

Reader 1:

The prince walked like one who was still asleep. He paid little attention to Kate as she followed him.

Reader 2:

The prince walked out the door of the castle into the stableyard where his horse stood saddled.

Reader 1:

He called his hound and jumped into his saddle. It was all like a dream.

Reader 2:

Kate watched for just the right moment, then she leapt lightly up onto the horse behind the prince.

Reader 1:

Away they rode through the forest. As they rode, Kate kept putting the nuts that grew on the trees into her apron.

Reader 2:

They rode on until they came to a green hill. The horse stopped as if he knew the place.

Reader 1:

The prince said, "Open, open green hill, let the young prince in with his horse and his hound and his lady up behind him."

Reader 2:

The green hill opened. They passed inside, and the prince and Kate slipped off the horse.

Reader 1:

They were in a splendid hall which was brightly lighted. Beautiful ladies, who looked like fairies, crowded round the prince. They led him away to dance.

From *Fairy Tales for Two Readers.* © 1995. Teacher Ideas Press. (800) 237-6124.

Reader 2:

Nobody noticed Kate as she hid behind the door. She watched for a long time.

Reader 1:

The prince danced and danced. Finally he fell, almost fainting upon a couch. Kate saw the fairy ladies fan the prince. Then he arose from the couch and went on dancing.

Reader 2:

Suddenly a cock crowed. The prince quickly mounted his horse.

Reader 1:

Kate managed to swing up behind him without being seen. Home they rode.

Reader 2:

The next morning the attendants found the prince lying pale in his bed. Kate was sitting by the fire, cracking nuts.

Reader 1:

Kate turned to the attendant and said, "The prince had a good night. If you will give me a peck of gold, I will be glad to sit with him another night."

Reader 2:

As Kate was the first person ever to stay the entire night, her wish was granted.

Reader 1:

The second night was like the first. The prince got up at midnight as if he were in a dream. He rode away to the green hill and the fairy ball.

Reader 2:

Once more Kate went with him. She gathered nuts as they rode through the forest. She hid behind the door, but this time she didn't watch the prince dance and dance.

Reader 1:

Kate looked about and noticed a fairy baby playing with a wand. She overheard one of the fairy ladies talking.

Reader 2:

The fairy lady said that three strokes of the wand would make Kate's sick sister, Princess Anne, as beautiful as ever.

Reader 1:

Kate had an idea. She rolled one nut after the other to the fairy baby. The baby began to toddle after the nuts. As the baby toddled after the nuts, she dropped the wand.

Reader 2:

Quickly Kate picked up the wand and hid it in her apron.

Reader 1:

When the cock crowed, the prince and Kate mounted the horse and rode home. When they reached home, Kate jumped off the horse. She rushed to Anne's room and touched her three times with the wand.

Reader 2:

When Kate touched Anne the third time, the nasty sheep's head fell off. Anne was her own pretty self again. The sisters were very happy.

Reader 1:

Unfortunately the poor prince was no better. The king was so sad!

Reader 2:

He asked Kate to sit by the prince's bedside another night.

Reader 1:

Kate said, "I'll be glad to sit with the prince if you will give me permission to marry him when he's well."

Reader 2:

Of course, the king agreed. What else could he do?

Reader 1:

The third night was like the first two. This time, though, the fairy baby was playing with a dead bird that had beautiful colored feathers.

Reader 2:

Kate overheard the fairy lady say, "Three bites of that beautiful bird would make the sick prince as well as ever!"

Reader 1:

Again Kate rolled nuts to the fairy baby. At last the baby toddled off after the rolling nuts and dropped the bird. Kate quickly picked up the bird and put it in her apron.

Reader 2:

When the cock crowed, Kate and the prince set off for home again. This time Kate didn't sit cracking nuts by the fire.

Reader 1:

She began plucking feathers and blowing up the fire.

Reader 2:

She cooked the bird. Soon there arose a delicious smell.

Reader 1:

The sick prince awakened and said, "Oh, I wish I had a bite of that birdie."

Reader 2:

Kate cut off a piece of the bird and gave him a bite. When he had eaten it, he propped himself up on his elbow.

Reader 1:

Kate went on with her roasting. By and by the prince cried out again, "Oh, if I could have another bite of that birdie!"

Reader 2:

Kate gave him another bite. With the second bite, the prince sat up in bed.

Reader 1:

"Oh, if I could just have a third bite of that birdie," the prince pleaded.

Reader 2:

Kate gave him a third bite. When he had eaten it, he rose up as strong as ever. He sat by the fire with Kate.

Reader 1:

When the royal family came in the next morning, they found Kate and the young prince very happy.

Reader 2:

In the meantime, the brother of the sick prince met Anne and fell in love with her.

Reader 1:

So, the sick son married the well sister, and the well son married the sick sister.

Reader 2:

They all lived happily and died happily!

Glossary

cock a rooster; any male bird

crockery pots and dishes

fairy a small, magical being

fast to not eat food

henwife a woman who raises poultry

larder a place where meat and other foods are kept

linen a fabric made of flax fibers

peck a fourth of a bushel; a measure of capacity

stableyard the area surrounding a stable

toddle to walk with short steps

wand a slender rod sometimes waved by a magician

From *Fairy Tales for Two Readers*. © 1995. Teacher Ideas Press. (800) 237-6124.

King Thrushbeard

Story Introduction

In this fairy tale originally told by the Brothers Grimm, a proud, haughty princess mocks all her suitors. Her father, the king, hopes to teach her a lesson and decides that the first beggar who comes to his door will be the princess's husband. The princess gets a beggar; however, she also gets a surprise.

Reader 1:

Once upon a time there was a king who had a beautiful daughter.

Reader 2:

Yes, indeed, she was very pretty. She was also very proud and haughty.

Reader 1:

Many men came to woo this beautiful young woman. None of them was good enough for her.

Reader 2:

She turned the men away, one after the other. She even mocked them.

Reader 1:

One day the king lined the suitors up according to their rank and position—kings, princes, dukes, earls, barons.

Reader 2:

The princess was led through the ranks. She found fault with each man.

Reader 1:

One was too stout.

Reader 2:

The next was too tall.

Reader 1:

One was too short.

Reader 2:

Another was too pale.

Reader 1:

The next was too ruddy.

Reader 2:

Another was not straight.

Reader 1:

The princess found something wrong with every one of them. She even insulted a king, who stood at the head of the row.

Reader 2:

"He has a chin like the beak of a thrush! I'll call him King Thrushbeard," she taunted.

Reader 1:

At last the king saw how ugly his daughter was on the inside. Her behavior made him very angry.

Reader 2:

He decided to punish his daughter. He said the first beggar who came to the door would be her husband.

Reader 1:

A few days later, a wandering musician began to sing outside the king's house. The king asked that he be brought into the royal chambers.

Reader 2:

The musician entered. He was dressed in dirty rags. He sang for the king and his daughter. Then he asked for alms.

Reader 1:

"I like your song so much that I will give you my daughter as your wife," said the king.

Reader 2:

The princess was beside herself. "Me, marry a beggar!"

Reader 1:

"I made an oath," said the king, "to give you to the first beggar who came. I will keep my word."

Reader 2:

A minister was brought to the castle. The princess was married to the beggar musician.

Reader 1:

"Now you are also a beggar," said the king. "You must go away with your husband!"

Reader 2:

The beggar took the princess by the hand and left with her on foot.

Reader 1:

Soon they came to a vast wood.

Reader 2:

"Who is the lord of this fine forest?" asked the princess.

Reader 1:

"It belongs to King Thrushbeard. It might have been yours if you had become his queen."

Reader 2:

"Sad must I sing," sighed the princess. "Oh, how I wish I'd accepted the hand of the king."

Reader 1:

Soon they reached a large meadow.

Reader 2:

"Who is the lord of this fine meadow?" asked the princess.

Reader 1:

"It belongs to King Thrushbeard. It might have been yours if you had become his queen," answered the beggar musician.

Reader 2:

"Sad must I sing," sighed the princess. "Oh, how I wish I'd accepted the hand of the king!"

Reader 1:

Soon they passed through a large city.

Reader 2:

"Who is the lord of this city?"

Reader 1:

Again the answer, "It belongs to King Thrushbeard. It might have been yours if you had become his queen."

Reader 2:

"Sad must I sing," sighed the princess. "Oh, how I wish I'd accepted the hand of the king!"

Reader 1:

"It makes me sad," said the wandering musician. "You're always wishing for another husband. Am I not good enough for you?"

Reader 2:

At last they came to a miserable little hovel. "Whose wretched little house is this?" asked the princess.

Reader 1:

"This is my house and yours," said the musician. "Here we will live together. Since the door is very low, stoop down to get inside your new home."

Reader 2:

"Where are the servants?" asked the princess.

Reader 1:

"Whatever is done, you must do for yourself. Light the fire and put on the kettle. I'm tired and hungry!"

From *Fairy Tales for Two Readers*. © 1995. Teacher Ideas Press. (800) 237-6124.

Reader 2:

The princess knew nothing about lighting fires and cooking. Finally the musician had to build the fire and cook for himself.

Reader 1:

The next morning the musician made the princess get up very early to do the housework.

Reader 2:

The princess, however, had never learned to work. Besides, she was lazy.

Reader 1:

Finally the musician said, "Wife, this won't do any longer. You can't live here without working. You will have to make baskets."

Reader 2:

The musician cut some willows so the princess could weave baskets. As she weaved, the hard willows bruised her tender hands.

Reader 1:

"That won't do," said the musician. "You had better spin. Maybe you can do that without hurting yourself."

Reader 2:

The princess sat down and tried to spin. Soon the harsh yarn cut her delicate fingers and made them bleed.

Reader 1:

The musician shouted, "Just look at you! There's nothing you can do! I certainly made a bad bargain when I got you! I will try to start an earthenware business. Surely you can sit in the market and sell my pots!"

Reader 2:

"Oh, I don't want to do that. The people from my father's kingdom will come and see me sitting in the marketplace. They'll laugh at me. I don't want to sell pots," pleaded the princess.

Reader 1:

Actually the princess had no choice. It was sell the goods or starve!

Reader 2:

She was so pretty that everybody wanted to buy her earthenware.

Reader 1:

They were able to live fairly well on the money the princess made selling her husband's pots.

Reader 2:

One day while she was sitting in the corner of the market, a drunken man came riding up on a beautiful horse. He rode right in among the pots, breaking them into a thousand pieces.

Reader 1:

The princess began to cry. She was sorry for her bad behavior. Why could she not have been as pretty on the inside as she was on the outside?

Reader 2:

"What will become of me? What will my husband say to me?" She ran home and told him of her misfortune.

Reader 1:

"Who would think just sitting at the corner of the market with crockery would be so difficult? You just stop that crying. I went down to the king's palace to find you a job. They need a kitchen servant. Surely you can do that! At least you will get your food free."

Reader 2:

The princess became a kitchen maid. She had to wait upon the cook and do all the dirty work.

Reader 1:

She put a pot in each of her pockets. In the pots she put her share of the scraps to take home.

Reader 2:

The day the king's sister was getting married, the kitchen maid went upstairs and stood behind the door to peek at all the splendor.

Reader 1:

When the rooms were lighted, she saw the guests streaming in. Each one was more beautiful than the other.

Reader 2:

She thought, with a heavy heart, of her sad fate.

Reader 1:

She cursed the pride and haughtiness that had caused all her problems.

Reader 2:

Suddenly King Thrushbeard came in. He was dressed in silk and velvet. He had a golden chain around his neck.

Reader 1:

When he saw the beautiful young woman standing at the door, he grabbed her hand. He wanted to dance with her.

Reader 2:

She refused to dance with him. Then she realized it was King Thrushbeard who had asked her to dance.

Reader 1:

King Thrushbeard dragged her into the hall. The string holding her pockets broke! Down fell the pots! The soup and savory morsels were spilled all over the floor.

Reader 2:

The guests began to laugh.

Reader 1:

The young woman was so ashamed. She wished the floor would swallow her.

Reader 2:

She rushed to the door to escape. King Thrushbeard, who was standing on the stairs, stopped her.

Reader 1:

He said, "Don't be afraid. The beggar musician and I are one and the same. I disguised myself because I love you. I was the rider who ran over your pots. I did all this to bend your proud spirit. I punished you for your haughtiness."

Reader 2:

The princess wept bitterly. "I was wicked! I am sorry for my bad behavior. I will try to be worthy of your love!"

Reader 1:

"Be happy," said the King. "Those evil days are over. We will celebrate our true wedding!"

Reader 2:

The ladies-in-waiting placed rich clothing on the princess. Her father came with his court and wished her joy in her marriage to King Thrushbeard.

Reader 1:

Finally the happiness began.

Reader 2:

The princess who had always been beautiful on the outside was finally beautiful on the inside.

Glossary

alms   gifts for the poor

crockery   pots and dishes

earthenware   dishes and pots made of baked clay

haughty   appreciating oneself and having disdain for others

hovel   a small hut

morsel   a small piece

ruddy   tinged with red

savory   of a good taste or odor

stout   strong; sound; tough

suitor   a man who courts a woman

swineherd   one who tends swine or hogs

taunt   to mock or make fun of

thrush   a migratory bird

woo   to court or seek the affection of another

wretched   poor or miserable

Mother Holly

Story Introduction

In the story "Mother Holly," adapted from one of the Brother Grimm fairy tales, Mother Holly rewards the widow's daughter who is kind and hardworking with a shower of gold. She rewards the lazy daughter with a shower of pitch. The widow learns a valuable lesson: to love both her daughters equally and to value kindness as gold.

Reader 1:

Once upon a time, there was a widow who had two daughters. One of them was very good and kind.

Reader 2:

The other was wicked and lazy, but she was the one the mother loved most.

Reader 1:

The kind daughter had to do all the housework. She had to sit by the well and spin until her fingers were sore.

Reader 2:

One day the poor young woman worked so long her fingers began to bleed. Some blood fell on her spindle.

Reader 1:

She leaned over the well and tried to wash the blood off. The spindle fell out of her hand and into the well.

Reader 2:

She ran home to tell her mother. She knocked on the door, but her mother and sister would not let her in. Her mother yelled at her for being so careless.

Reader 1:

"You let the spindle fall into the well! You must go and get it! Don't come back without it!"

Reader 2:

The kind daughter went back to the well. She did not know what to do. She could not reach the spindle.

Reader 1:

Finally she jumped into the well and sank down into the deep water.

Reader 2:

She found herself in a beautiful meadow.

Reader 1:

The sun was shining. There were beautiful flowers blooming as far as she could see.

Reader 2:

The young woman walked across the meadow. Soon she came to a baker's oven full of bread.

Reader 1:

The loaves cried out to her, "Take us out! Take us out! We will be burned! We were baked long ago!"

Reader 2:

She picked up the bread shovel and took the bread from the oven.

Reader 1:

She travelled on a little further. She came to a tree full of apples.

Reader 2:

"Shake me, shake me, I pray! My apples are all ripe and my back is breaking!" the tree begged.

Reader 1:

The kind daughter shook the tree. The apples came falling down. Soon there was not a single apple left on the tree.

Reader 2:

She put the apples in a basket and walked on again.

Reader 1:

Next she came to a pretty little house. She saw an old woman looking out the window.

Reader 2:

The old woman was smiling. Her teeth were large. The young woman was afraid.

Reader 1:

"Don't be afraid, my child! I am old Mother Holly. Come and stay with me. If you will help me with my house, I will make you very happy. Be very careful when you make my bed. Always shake it very hard. Make the feathers fly. Down in the world, they will say it is snowing."

Reader 2:

The old woman seemed so nice that the kind daughter agreed to work for her.

Reader 1:

She tried to do everything just like the old woman wanted. When she made Mother Holly's bed, she shook it with all her might.

Reader 2:

The feathers flew about like snowflakes. Down in the world, they said it was snowing.

Reader 1:

The old woman never spoke angrily to the kind daughter. Every day she gave her good things to eat.

Reader 2:

The young woman stayed on with Mother Holly for some time. After a while, she became unhappy.

Reader 1:

At first she did not know why she was unhappy. Finally she realized she was homesick. She turned to Mother Holly.

Reader 2:

"Mother Holly, I am homesick. I cannot stay with you any longer. You have been kind to me, but I need to go home."

Reader 1:

"I am surprised you would want to go back to your own family, my dear. You have done a good job so I will take you part of the way myself," answered Mother Holly.

Reader 2:

She led the young woman through a wide gate. As the young woman passed through, a shower of gold fell upon her. The gold was all about her. She was shining with it from head to toe.

Reader 1:

"That is your reward for your kindness and hard work. Here's the spindle you dropped. Good-bye! Take care!" said Mother Holly.

Reader 2:

The young woman found herself in the field behind her mother's house. She entered the yard. The rooster crowed.

Reader 1:

"Cock-a-doodle doo! Your golden daughter's come back to you!"

Reader 2:

The kind daughter was covered in gold. Her mother and sister gave her a warm welcome. She told them her story.

Reader 1:

The mother listened carefully to the story about how her daughter earned her riches. She wanted her other daughter—the wicked, lazy daughter—to seek her fortune.

Reader 2:

So, she sent the lazy daughter to sit by the well and spin. But, the young woman was too lazy to spin.

Reader 1:

Instead, she stuck her hand into a thorn bush. A drop of blood from her pricked finger fell on the spindle. She threw the spindle into the well and jumped in.

Reader 2:

Like her sister, the lazy daughter awoke in the beautiful meadow. She walked until she came to the oven.

Reader 1:

The loaves of bread begged her to take them out of the oven before they were burned.

Reader 2:

"Do you think I'm going to dirty my hands with the likes of you?" the young woman asked.

Reader 1:

She walked proudly on until she came to the apple tree.

Reader 2:

"Shake me! Shake me, I pray! My apples are all ripe! My back is breaking!" the tree begged.

Reader 1:

The wicked young woman was too proud to even consider helping the apple tree.

Reader 2:

"A nice thing to ask me to do. One of your apples might fall on my head!" she answered. She hurried on until she came to Mother Holly's house.

Reader 1:

Her sister had told her all about the old woman's large teeth, so the lazy daughter was not afraid. Right away she agreed to work for Mother Holly.

Reader 2:

The first day the lazy young woman worked hard to please Mother Holly. She thought of the gold she would get in return.

Reader 1:

The next day she began to slow down. She did not work very hard. The third day, she was lazier still.

Reader 2:

Soon she began to lie in bed until late in the day. She did not want to get up. She would not make the old woman's bed properly. She would not shake it so the feathers flew about.

From *Fairy Tales for Two Readers*. © 1995. Teacher Ideas Press. (800) 237-6124.

Reader 1:

Mother Holly quickly got tired of her. She soon wanted to be rid of the lazy young woman. This news made the young woman happy. The gold, she thought, would soon be hers.

Reader 2:

Mother Holly led her to the wide gate. The lazy daughter passed through. A big bucket of pitch poured on her.

Reader 1:

"This is in return for your services. Go, I am shutting my gate behind you!" shouted Mother Holly.

Reader 2:

The lazy young woman had to go home covered with pitch. She entered the yard. The rooster crowed.

Reader 1:

"Cock-a-doodle doo! Cock-a-doodle doo! Your dirty daughter has come back to you!"

Reader 2:

The pitch stuck to the lazy daughter for a long, long time. By the time she had cleaned it off, she had mended her ways. She became as good and kind as her sister.

Reader 1:

Their mother saw then that it was kindness that was golden. She loved both her daughters equally, and they all lived happily ever after.

Glossary

pitch   a thick, dark, tar-like substance

spindle   a slender rod on a spinning wheel that holds the spool around which the thread is wound

---

Mr. and Mrs. Vinegar

Story Introduction

This story, adapted from one of Joseph Jacobs's English fairy tales, relates the adventures of Mr. and Mrs. Vinegar. After Mrs. Vinegar breaks their vinegar bottle house, they must go out into the world to seek their fortune. Mr. Vinegar squanders away a fortune before he and his wife finally find a simple, little home—another vinegar bottle. All is well that ends well, and Mr. Vinegar learns to spend his money more wisely.

Reader 1:

Mr. and Mrs. Vinegar lived in a vinegar bottle.

Reader 2:

Mrs. Vinegar was a very tidy person.

Reader 1:

One day, while she was busy sweeping her vinegar bottle house, she hit the wall with her broomstick.

Reader 2:

Crash! Down came her whole house in bits. Clitter clatter!

Reader 1:

Mrs. Vinegar was nearly buried in broken glass.

Reader 2:

She rushed out to find Mr. Vinegar.

Reader 1:

"Oh, Mr. Vinegar, such a dreadful thing has happened! We're ruined! I've hit the wall with the end of my broom. Now the whole house is smashed into little pieces."

Reader 2:

He answered, "We'll just have to do the best we can, my dearie. We'll just go out into the world to seek our fortune. Look here, the door is still in good shape. I will put it on my back and take it along with us. It's sure to come in handy."

Reader 1:

Off they went down the road. When night came, they were tired. They were near a thick forest.

Reader 2:

"My love, I'll climb up in that tree over there. I'll pull the door up after me and wedge it safe on that strong branch. You climb up after me. We'll be able to sleep safely," said Mr. Vinegar.

Reader 1:

This was done. The two stretched themselves out carefully on the door and went to sleep.

Reader 2:

In the middle of the night, they were awakened by the sound of voices under the tree.

Reader 1:

"Here's five pounds for you, Jack."

Reader 2:

"Thank you, Captain!"

Reader 1:

"Here's three pounds for you, Bill."

Reader 2:

Bill was not pleased. In fact, he felt cheated that he had not been given as much money as Jack.

Reader 1:

The voices went on. The Captain said, "Bob, you get ten pounds for your share."

Reader 2:

Mr. and Mrs. Vinegar began to feel more and more uneasy.

Reader 1:

They decided the men under the tree must be a gang of robbers who were busy dividing up money they had stolen.

Reader 2:

Because Mr. and Mrs. Vinegar were respectable folks, this idea frightened them. They began to shake and tremble.

Reader 1:

The door wasn't very firmly wedged. It fell, thump, right on the heads of the robbers.

Reader 2:

Clinging to the branches for dear life, Mr. and Mrs. Vinegar perched up in the tree and hoped the robbers would not find them.

Reader 1:

Of course, now it was the robbers' turn to be afraid. Away they ran.

Reader 2:

Mr. and Mrs. Vinegar didn't know for certain the robbers had gone. They didn't dare come down out of the tree until daylight.

Reader 1:

At last Mr. Vinegar climbed down carefully. He lifted the door. There on the ground were all the golden guineas the frightened robbers had left behind.

Reader 2:

"Come down, Mrs. Vinegar. Come down! Our fortune's made!"

Reader 1:

Mrs. Vinegar came down as fast as she could. Oh, how pleased she was at the sight of all that money!

From *Fairy Tales for Two Readers.* © 1995. Teacher Ideas Press. (800) 237-6124.

Reader 2:

They quickly counted the money and found to their delight they had forty guineas.

Reader 1:

"My dear, I'll tell you what we will do. You take the money to the fair and buy a cow," said Mrs. Vinegar. "I know how to make splendid butter and cheese. We then could sell our wares and make a fine living."

Reader 2:

Mr. Vinegar took the money and went to the fair to buy a cow.

Reader 1:

He wasn't at the fair very long before he saw a beautiful red cow. She seemed to be an excellent milker, too.

Reader 2:

"Oh, what a beautiful cow! If only I had that cow, I would be the happiest man alive!" thought Mr. Vinegar.

Reader 1:

He offered to pay his whole forty guineas for that cow, despite the fact that the cow was worth much less.

Reader 2:

Even though she was a good cow and a good milker, it wasn't at all wise of Mr. Vinegar to pay that much money for her.

Reader 1:

Of course, the man who was selling the cow would not tell Mr. Vinegar he was paying too much. He praised the cow a great deal. Then he pretended he was selling the cow for so little just because he liked Mr. Vinegar.

Reader 2:

Silly old Mr. Vinegar turned over all his money to the man. Then he led the cow away.

Reader 1:

The rest of the fair was going on all around.

Reader 2:

Mr. Vinegar and his big, red cow joined in the merriment.

Reader 1:

Soon Mr. Vinegar saw a man who was playing the bagpipes. Oh, what a fine noise the man made!

Reader 2:

All the children were following the piper around. People were throwing money into his cup.

Reader 1:

Mr. Vinegar listened and looked. He thought the man and his bagpipes were wonderful.

Reader 2:

"Oh, what a splendid way to make a living! I'd be the happiest man alive if I had your bagpipes. Those are wonderful bagpipes. And you make so much money," said Mr. Vinegar.

Reader 1:

"Yes, they really are wonderful bagpipes. I do make a lot of money. I live a fine life," admitted the piper.

Reader 2:

"How about if I give you my beautiful red cow for those bagpipes?" asked Mr. Vinegar.

Reader 1:

"Well, okay," said the piper. It was a very good deal for him.

Reader 2:

As you probably guessed, Mr. Vinegar hadn't the foggiest notion how to play those bagpipes. He puffed! He blew! He squeezed and squeezed!

Reader 1:

All he could get out of those bagpipes was a doleful, direful screeching and groaning.

From *Fairy Tales for Two Readers*. © 1995. Teacher Ideas Press. (800) 237-6124.

Reader 2:

The people certainly didn't crowd around and give him money.

Reader 1:

The adults hurried off as fast as they could.

Reader 2:

The children threw mud at him. There was nothing left for Mr. Vinegar to do but go away.

Reader 1:

The day began to cloud over and grow chilly. Poor Mr. Vinegar began to feel cold. Just as he began to think about how cold he was, he met a man who was wearing a pair of nice, thick gloves.

Reader 2:

"Oh, how cold my hands are. If I only had a pair of nice, thick gloves, I would be the happiest man alive!" cried Mr. Vinegar.

Reader 1:

"You know, it has turned cold. And yet, with these gloves, my hands are as warm as toast," boasted the man.

Reader 2:

"I sure wish I had a pair of gloves like yours," admitted Mr. Vinegar.

Reader 1:

"Well, I'll trade them to you for that pair of bagpipes," said the man.

Reader 2:

"Done," said Mr. Vinegar. "Oh, what a nice pair of gloves!"

Reader 1:

For a while Mr. Vinegar was very happy as he went on his way back to Mrs. Vinegar.

Reader 2:

It was a long walk home. Soon he began to feel tired. His legs ached.

Reader 1:

About that time, he saw a man walking along with a good stout stick.

Reader 2:

"That sure is a good stick you've got there. If I had a stick like that, I'd be the happiest man alive," said Mr. Vinegar.

Reader 1:

"It is a good stick. It's been a good friend to me for many a long mile. I don't mind letting you have it in exchange for that pair of warm gloves you are wearing," said the man.

Reader 2:

"Done!" said Mr. Vinegar. "I'll just take off these gloves and give them to you for that stick."

Reader 1:

As he walked along and got nearer home, Mr. Vinegar began to look at that stick and then at the hedges along the road.

Reader 2:

There were sticks on those hedges just as good as the one for which he'd traded his gloves.

Reader 1:

After that, he began to think over all the bargains he'd made that day.

Reader 2:

He'd started out with forty guineas and ended up with a stick.

Reader 1:

And that stick was no better than one he could have cut for himself out of the bushes.

Reader 2:

Just as he was thinking all this, a jay, calling, "Ha! Ha! Ha! Ha!" came flying through the trees.

Reader 1:

The jay sounded exactly as if it were laughing at Mr. Vinegar.

Reader 2:

"You impudent bird! How dare you laugh at me!" screamed Mr. Vinegar.

Reader 1:

With that, he threw his stick at the bird, which flew away, ha-hawing all the more.

Reader 2:

The stick lodged in one of the tree branches. Mr. Vinegar tried to climb the tree to get it. He tried to shake it down, but all in vain.

Reader 1:

When Mr. Vinegar finally arrived home, he had nothing at all to show Mrs. Vinegar for the forty guineas.

Reader 2:

He sat down on the ground beside Mrs. Vinegar. They just looked and looked at each other. Some people say that they're both sitting there to this day.

Reader 1:

But others say that after that, Mr. Vinegar grew wiser. He and Mrs. Vinegar found another vinegar bottle that someone had thrown away. They managed to set up their house again.

Glossary

direful   terrible; warning of disaster

doleful   mournful

guinea   an English gold coin, worth one pound and one shilling

hedge   bushes set close together

impudent   unwise

piper   one who plays a reed musical instrument

pound   the standard monetary unit of the United Kingdom

respectable   one who is loved and trusted

squander   to waste

wares   goods; merchandise

wedge   to tighten something in place by forcing it into a small space

---

From *Fairy Tales for Two Readers.* © 1995. Teacher Ideas Press. (800) 237-6124.

The Seven Ravens

Story Introduction

In the Brothers Grimm fairy tale "The Seven Ravens," a father becomes discontent with his seven sons because the boys fail to respond quickly to his requests. The father wishes his sons would turn into ravens. His wish is granted, as seven black birds fly away. The boys are rescued from their unhappy fate by their brave, little sister, and the father learns to be careful about his wishes for they just may come true.

Reader 1:

Once there was a man who had seven sons but no daughter.

Reader 2:

Oh, how he wished for a little girl!

Reader 1:

Finally his joy was complete. He and his wife had a daughter.

Reader 2:

The little girl was small and delicate, so they decided to christen her at home.

Reader 1:

The man sent one of his sons to the spring to get some water.

Reader 2:

The other six boys ran with him. Each wanted to be the first to draw the water.

Reader 1:

As they pushed each other, the pitcher fell into the brook.

Reader 2:

The boys did not know what to do. They were afraid to go home.

Reader 1:

When they didn't return, the father grew impatient.

Reader 2:

"Those rascals must be playing. They must have forgotten why they went to the spring!"

Reader 1:

The father was afraid the frail, little girl would die before she was christened.

Reader 2:

He was so angry he cried, "I wish those boys would turn into ravens!"

Reader 1:

Suddenly the father heard a whirring sound in the air above his head.

Reader 2:

He looked up to see seven coal-black ravens flying away.

Reader 1:

The man and his wife could not undo the spell. They were very sad about the loss of their seven sons.

Reader 2:

They tried to console themselves with the love of the little daughter, who grew strong and beautiful.

Reader 1:

For a long time, the little girl did not know she had any brothers.

Reader 2:

One day she heard someone say, "She certainly is pretty. But you know she is really to blame for the misfortune of her seven brothers."

Reader 1:

The girl became very sad. She asked her mother and father if it were true that she had seven brothers.

Reader 2:

Her parents could no longer keep the secret. They tried to tell her that what happened to the boys was not her fault.

Reader 1:

The girl could not stop thinking about her brothers. She was determined to set them free.

Reader 2:

She set off into the world to find and free her brothers.

Reader 1:

She took nothing with her but a little ring as a remembrance of her parents, a loaf of bread to fight hunger, a pitcher of water to prevent thirst, and a little chair in which to rest.

Reader 2:

She traveled on and on until she came to the end of the world.

Reader 1:

She traveled to the sun. It was hot and terrible. It devoured little children.

Reader 2:

She ran quickly over to the moon. It was cold, dismal, and dreary.

Reader 1:

While she was looking at the moon, it said, "I smell human flesh!"

Reader 2:

Then she ran quickly to the stars. They were kind and good. Each one sat on its own special seat.

Reader 1:

The morning star stood up and gave the girl a little bone.

Reader 2:

"Unless you have this bone, you cannot open the glass mountain," said the morning star. "Your brothers are on the glass mountain."

Reader 1:

The girl wrapped the bone carefully in a little kerchief.

Reader 2:

She travelled to the glass mountain.

Reader 1:

The gate was closed. She opened the handkerchief.

Reader 2:

It was empty. She had lost the little bone.

Reader 1:

What could she do? She had no key.

Reader 2:

She was determined, though, to rescue her brothers.

Reader 1:

She took a knife and cut off her own tiny finger.

Reader 2:

She placed the bone of her own finger in the keyhole. The lock clicked, and the door opened.

Reader 1:

As she entered, she met a dwarf.

Reader 2:

"My child, who or what are you trying to find?" asked the dwarf.

Reader 1:

"I am looking for my brothers, the seven ravens," she answered.

Reader 2:

"My masters, the ravens, are not at home," said the dwarf. "Have a seat and wait for them."

Reader 1:

The dwarf brought in supper for the ravens. He filled seven little plates and seven little cups.

Reader 2:

The sister took a crumb or two from each plate. She took a sip from each little cup.

Reader 1:

She let her ring fall into the last little cup. Almost at once she heard a whirring and crying in the air.

Reader 2:

"The ravens are coming home," said the dwarf.

Reader 1:

The ravens came in and immediately wanted to eat and drink. They looked at their little plates and cups.

Reader 2:

They said one after another, "Look here. Someone has eaten off my plate! Who has been drinking out of my cup? There has been a human mouth here."

Reader 1:

The seventh raven drank to the bottom of his cup. The ring rolled up against his beak.

Reader 2:

"This ring belongs to our mother and father," he said. Then they all began talking at once, "Please let our sister be here. Please let her free us!"

Reader 1:

The girl was standing behind the door listening. She overheard all they said.

Reader 2:

As the girl came forward, the ravens returned to their human form. They were very happy to see their little sister.

Reader 1:

And they all lived happily ever after.

Glossary

christen   to name a child as part of a baptismal ceremony

console   to comfort

devour   to eat up greedily

dismal   cheerless; depressing

dreary   sad or gloomy appearing

frail   weak

kerchief   a woman's square scarf, often worn on her head

rascal   one who gets into trouble

remembrance   an object to remind one of something or someone

The
Six Servants

Story Introduction

The Brothers Grimm fairy tale "The Six Servants" tells of a prince who meets six servants while he travels to another country to win the hand of a beautiful princess. They outsmart the princess's mother, a sorceress, and with the help of his new friends, the prince marries a woman who becomes as beautiful in her heart as in her outward appearance.

Reader 1:

In olden times there was a wicked queen who was also a sorceress.

Reader 2:

The queen had a daughter who was the most beautiful maiden under the sun.

Reader 1:

Many men were dazzled by the daughter's beauty.

Reader 2:

Each time a man came asking for the daughter's hand in marriage, the queen demanded he perform a task she was certain he could not accomplish.

Reader 1:

Those who tried for the beautiful daughter's hand in marriage usually lost their lives.

Reader 2:

A king's son from another country heard of the maiden's beauty.

Reader 1:

He begged, "Let me go there, Father. I want to demand the beautiful maiden's hand in marriage."

Reader 2:

"Never," said the king, "you would be going to your death."

Reader 1:

When the prince heard this, he fell deathly ill!

Reader 2:

He lay near death's door for seven years. The doctors could not heal him.

Reader 1:

Finally, when the father had no other hope for his son's recovery, he gave in.

Reader 2:

"Go! Try your luck. I know of no other means of curing you."

Reader 1:

The son rose from his bed, and like magic, he was well again. He immediately set on his way to the queen's palace.

Reader 2:

As the prince rode along, he saw from afar something that looked like a great heap of hay lying on the ground.

Reader 1:

When he got nearer, he saw that it was a man with a large stomach, lying down in the road.

Reader 2:

"If you are in need of anyone, take me into your service," said Big Man.

Reader 1:

"What can I do with such a clumsy person?" asked the prince.

Reader 2:

"When I really puff myself up, I am a thousand times bigger," boasted Big Man.

Reader 1:

"If that's the case, I can make use of you. Come with me, Big Man," said the prince.

Reader 2:

Big Man followed the prince. After a while they found another person lying on the ground with his ear pressed to the turf.

Reader 1:

"What are you doing there?" asked the prince.

Reader 2:

"I am listening," said Sharp Ears.

Reader 1:

"Why are you listening so attentively?" asked the prince.

Reader 2:

"I am listening to what is going on in the world, for nothing escapes my ears. I can even hear the grass growing."

Reader 1:

"Tell me what you hear at the court of the old queen who has the beautiful daughter," said the prince.

Reader 2:

"I hear the whizzing of the sword that is striking off a lover's head."

Reader 1:

"I can make use of you, Sharp Ears. Come with me!" said the prince.

Reader 2:

Sharp Ears followed the prince. The three walked on for some distance. After a time, they saw a pair of legs, but the man was so tall they could hardly see the rest of his body.

Reader 1:

"Why, what a tall rascal you are!" exclaimed the prince.

Reader 2:

"Oh, that's nothing at all. When I really stretch out my limbs, I am a thousand times as tall. I am taller than the highest mountain on earth. I will gladly enter your service, if you will take me," said Tall Man.

Reader 1:

"Come with me. I can make use of you, Tall Man," said the prince.

Reader 2:

Tall man also followed the prince. They went on and found a man sitting by the road. The man had bound up his eyes.

Reader 1:

"Do you have weak eyes? Is that the reason you can't look at the light?" asked the prince.

Reader 2:

"No, but I must not remove the bandage. With just one glance, I would split anything I looked at into pieces. If you can use such a powerful pair of eyes, I will be glad to serve you," said Sharp Eyes.

Reader 1:

"Come with me! I can make use of you, Sharp Eyes!" said the prince.

Reader 2:

Sharp Eyes joined the travellers. They journeyed on until they found a man lying in the hot sunshine. He was trembling and shivering all over. Not a limb was still.

Reader 1:

"How can you shiver when the sun is shining so warm?" asked the prince.

Reader 2:

"Alas, I am of a different nature. The hotter it is, the colder I am. The frost pierces through all my bones! The colder it is, the hotter I am. In the midst of ice, I cannot endure the heat. In the midst of fire, I cannot endure the cold," said Frosty Man.

Reader 1:

"You are a strange fellow, but I would like you to enter my service and follow me, Frosty Man!" said the prince.

Reader 2:

Frosty Man followed the prince. The companions travelled on. Soon they saw a man who had an unusually long neck. When he looked about him, he could see over all the mountains.

Reader 1:

"What are you looking at so eagerly?" asked the prince.

Reader 2:

"I have such a long neck that I can see into every forest and field and hill and valley, all over the world," said Long Neck.

Reader 1:

"Come with me, if you will. I can use a man with that talent," said the prince.

Reader 2:

Long Neck followed the prince. Finally the prince and his six servants came to the town where the old queen lived. They went to see the queen, but the prince didn't tell her who he was.

Reader 1:

"I am here to ask for the hand of your beautiful daughter. I will gladly perform any task you set for me," said the prince.

Reader 2:

Of course, the queen was delighted to get such a handsome youth as this into her net. She said, "I will give you three tasks. If you are able to perform them all, you shall be the husband of my daughter."

Reader 1:

"What is the first task?" asked the prince.

Reader 2:

"You must find the ring that I dropped into the ocean."

Reader 1:

The prince went home to his servants. "The first task is not easy. A ring must be brought up from the bottom of the ocean. Can you find some way of doing it?"

Reader 2:

"I will see where it is lying," said Long Neck. "Oh, yes, it is hanging there on a pointed stone."

Reader 1:

Tall Man said he could get it out if he could only see it.

Reader 2:

Big Man lay down and put his mouth to the water. He drank up the whole sea until it was as dry as a meadow.

Reader 1:

Tall Man stooped down a little and brought out the ring.

Reader 2:

The prince was so happy that he immediately took the ring to the old queen.

Reader 1:

The old queen was very surprised.

Reader 2:

"Well, yes, it is the right ring. You have performed the first task, but now comes the second. Do you see the meadow in front of my palace? Three hundred fat oxen are feeding there, and these must you eat, skin, hair, bones, horns, and all. Also, down below in my cellar lie three hundred casks of wine. You must drink these as well. If one hair of the oxen, or one single drop of the wine is left, your life will be forfeited to me."

Reader 1:

"May I invite guests? No dinner is good without some company," said the prince.

Reader 2:

"You may invite one for the sake of companionship, but no more," agreed the queen.

Reader 1:

The prince invited Big Man to be his guest.

Reader 2:

Big Man puffed himself up and ate the three hundred oxen without leaving one single hair. Then he asked if there was anything for supper.

Reader 1:

Next, Big Man drank all the wine straight from the casks without feeling any need for a glass.

Reader 2:

When the meal was over, the prince went to the old queen and told her the second task was also performed.

Reader 1:

The old queen admitted no one had ever done so much before.

Reader 2:

"There's still one remaining task. This night I will bring my daughter to you in your chamber. You must put your arms around her. As you sit together, do not fall asleep. When the clock strikes twelve, I will come. If my daughter is no longer in your arms, you are doomed," she said.

Reader 1:

The prince thought this task would be easy. Certainly he could keep his eyes open until midnight!

Reader 2:

He called his servants and told them what the old queen said.

Reader 1:

"Who knows what is behind this. I must be careful. Make sure the maiden does not go out of my room," the prince said.

Reader 2:

When night fell, the old queen came with her daughter.

Reader 1:

Tall Man wound himself around the two as they sat together.

Reader 2:

Big Man placed himself by the door so that no living creature could enter.

Reader 1:

As the prince and the maiden sat, the princess spoke not a word. Through the window, the moon shone on her face. The prince could see her beauty.

From *Fairy Tales for Two Readers*. © 1995. Teacher Ideas Press. (800) 237-6124.

Reader 2:

The prince sat gazing at her pretty face. He was filled with love and happiness. His eyes never felt weary.

Reader 1:

At eleven o'clock the old queen cast a sleeping spell over all of them. As soon as they fell asleep, the maiden was carried away.

Reader 2:

They all slept soundly until a quarter to twelve. When the magic lost its power, they all awakened.

Reader 1:

"Oh misery and misfortune! This is the end of me," said the prince.

Reader 2:

"I can see her," said Long Neck. "The princess is on an enchanted rock three hundred leagues from here. She is crying. You alone, Tall Man, can help her. If you will stand up, you will be there in a couple of steps."

Reader 1:

Tall Man was willing to help, but he needed Sharp Eyes to go with him and destroy the rock.

Reader 2:

Tall Man put Sharp Eyes on his back. In a flash they were on the enchanted rock.

Reader 1:

Tall Man removed the bandage of Sharp Eyes. Sharp Eyes looked around. The rock split into a thousand pieces.

Reader 2:

With Sharp Eyes on his back, Tall Man carried the maiden back in his arms.

Reader 1:

Before the clock struck twelve, they were all waiting for the queen.

Reader 2:

As the clock struck twelve, the queen thought, "Now he is mine!"

Reader 1:

When she saw her daughter in the prince's arms, the queen became alarmed.

Reader 2:

"Here is one who knows more than I do," she thought.

Reader 1:

The old queen dared not deny her promise. The prince had clearly won the hand of her daughter.

Reader 2:

In one last effort to cause the prince grief, the old queen whispered in her daughter's ear, "It is a disgrace for you to have to marry a commoner. It's a shame you were not allowed to choose a husband of your own liking."

Reader 1:

This made the princess angry, so she decided to take charge of her own destiny.

Reader 2:

The next morning she had three hundred bundles of wood stacked together. She challenged the prince.

Reader 1:

"You have performed the three tasks well. But I will not be your wife until someone seats himself in the middle of the wood while it is on fire."

Reader 2:

The princess did not believe any of the prince's servants would be burned for him.

Reader 1:

She thought the prince, out of love for her, would burn himself up in the fire. Then she would be free.

Reader 2:

The prince invited Frosty Man to sit in the middle of the fire which burned for three days.

Reader 1:

When the flames had burned all the wood, Frosty Man was standing amid the ashes, trembling like an aspen leaf.

Reader 2:

"I never felt such a frost during the whole course of my life. If it had lasted much longer, I would have been numbed!" cried Frosty Man.

Reader 1:

There was nothing else the beautiful maiden could do. She would become the wife of the prince.

Reader 2:

The furious, old queen said, "I cannot endure this disgrace!"

Reader 1:

She sent her warriors after the prince and her daughter. She ordered her warriors to bring the girl home.

Reader 2:

Sharp Ears heard what the old queen said.

Reader 1:

Big Man wanted to help the prince.

Reader 2:

Suddenly he knew what to do. He spat out seawater behind the carriage. A great lake arose. The warriors drowned.

Reader 1:

Then the old queen sent her knights.

Reader 2:

Again, Sharp Ears heard the rattling of their armor.

Reader 1:

Sharp Ears untied the bandage of Sharp Eyes. Sharp Eyes looked hard at the enemy troops, who shattered to pieces like glass.

Reader 2:

The prince and the beautiful maiden went on their way undisturbed. When the two were married and had been blessed in church, the six servants said, "Your wishes are now satisfied. You need us no longer. We will go our way and seek our fortunes."

From *Fairy Tales for Two Readers*. © 1995. Teacher Ideas Press. (800) 237-6124.

Reader 1:

As the prince and the princess travelled to his kingdom, they entered the village where the swineherd lived. The prince asked his bride, "Do you know who I really am? I am no prince, but a herder of swine, and the man who is there with that herd is my father. We must get to work and help him!"

Reader 2:

The prince carried his bride into the inn. He had the innkeeper take away her royal apparel during the night.

Reader 1:

When the young woman awakened in the morning, she had nothing to wear. The innkeeper's wife gave her an old gown and a pair of stockings.

Reader 2:

The princess really believed her husband was a swineherd.

Reader 1:

She resolved to help him herd the pigs. After all, he was a kind man.

Reader 2:

She reasoned that she had been haughty and proud. She decided she deserved the job. She was very sorry for her haughty behavior.

Reader 1:

She herded the pigs for a week. She soon had sores on her feet. She could not endure the hard work any longer.

Reader 2:

Finally the innkeeper asked the princess, "Do you know the true identity of your husband?"

Reader 1:

The maiden answered, "Yes, he is a swineherd. He is out in the field with the swine."

Reader 2:

The innkeeper had the servants take the princess to the palace.

From *Fairy Tales for Two Readers*. © 1995. Teacher Ideas Press. (800) 237-6124.

Reader 1:
There stood her husband, dressed in the king's cloak. He took the princess in his arms and kissed her. The wedding was celebrated!

Glossary

apparel   clothing

cask   a wooden vessel that is shaped like a barrel

chamber   a bedroom or room in a house

cloak   a loose outer garment, usually without sleeves

dazzle   to blind with bright light

endure   to carry on despite hardships

forfeit   to give something up as a penalty

haughty   appreciating oneself and having disdain for others

league   a distance equal to about three miles

pierce   to cut with a sharp object such as a knife

shatter   to break into many pieces

sorceress   a female magician

swine   a domesticated pig

swineherd   one who tends swine or hogs

tremble   to shake

turf   sod or grass with matted roots

warrior   a soldier

The Three Pigs

Story Introduction

"The Three Pigs," adapted from one of Joseph Jacobs's English fairy tales, is the story of three young pigs who go out into the world to seek their fortune. Several encounters with the big, bad wolf help prepare the pigs for life in the real world.

Reader 1:

One lovely day Mrs. Pig thought to herself, "Hmmm, I think it is time my three piglets went out into the world. They have played, eaten, and slept in my little house all these months. Now they must go and build new houses of their own."

Reader 2:

So Mrs. Pig awakened the piglets. She fed them a good breakfast, kissed them good-bye, and sent them out into the world on their own.

Reader 1:

The piglets went down the road together until they came to where the roads crossed. There they parted and went their separate ways.

Reader 2:

The first piglet said, "Now, let's see. Let me hurry and build my house so I can lie in the sun and play in the water hole. I'll just take the first thing I see and build a house. That fresh, sweet-smelling straw will do just fine. I will build my house of straw."

Reader 1:

In a short while, the first little pig had built his house. He went inside and ate another meal. He played with his new, red wagon. Then he lay down for a morning nap.

Reader 2:

In the meantime, the second piglet was also busy. "I must hurry and build myself a new house. Then I can eat and play and sleep all afternoon. These sticks will do just fine. I'll build my house of sticks."

Reader 1:

In an hour or two, his stick house was complete.

Reader 2:

A little further down the road, the third piglet was deciding what kind of house he would build. "Now, let's see. I want a strong house. I will build my house of bricks and stones. It will take me a long time to build my new house. But, when it's finished, it will be beautiful. I will be safe."

Reader 1:

The third piglet worked hard. Finally his beautiful house was finished. He went inside, locked his door, ate his dinner, and went to bed.

Reader 2:

While all three piglets slept, a hungry wolf came.

Reader 1:

"Snuff, snuff, I smell a piglet! There in that straw house must be my pig. Little pig, little pig, let me come in," yelled the wolf.

Reader 2:

"Not by the hair of my chinny-chin-chin," said the first piglet.

Reader 1:

"Then I'll huff, and I'll puff, and I'll blow your house in!" said the wolf.

Reader 2:

And he huffed, and he puffed, and he blew the house of straw into a heap. He looked in the straw for his supper pig, but the piglet was nowhere around.

Reader 1:

The little pig ran and ran. He ran to the house of sticks his brother had built.

Reader 2:

The wolf followed his nose. Soon he was pounding on the door of the second little pig.

Reader 1:

"Little pigs, little pigs, let me come in!" begged the hungry wolf.

Reader 2:

"Not by the hair of our chinny-chin-chins!" sang the little pigs.

Reader 1:

"Very well! I'll huff, and I'll puff, and I'll blow your house in!" warned the wolf.

Reader 2:

He huffed and he puffed. He blew the house into a pile of sticks. He looked for the little pigs. He found nothing but sticks.

Reader 1:

The little pigs ran as fast as they could. They ran to their brother's brick house. The third little pig quickly locked the door behind them.

Reader 2:

The two piglets began to tell their brother about the big, hungry wolf. Suddenly the wolf was beating at the door of the brick house.

Reader 1:

"Little pigs, little pigs, please let me come in! I want to visit with you. I want to show you my new ruby ring," begged the hungry old wolf.

Reader 2:

"Not by the hair of our chinny-chin-chins! We don't want to see you or your ruby ring. Go away!" yelled the pigs.

Reader 1:

"Then I'll huff, and I'll puff, and I'll blow your house in! Here I come," screamed the wolf.

Reader 2:

The wolf huffed and puffed and blew a strong wind. He could not move the house of bricks and stones.

Reader 1:

He blew and he blew and he blew. The house did not fall. The wolf became angrier and angrier!

Reader 2:

He scratched! He dug! He pounded! He ran around and around in a circle. He pushed! He jumped up and down! He had a roaring, running temper tantrum!

Reader 1:

"I'm going to get you yet. Yes, I will. I will huff and puff. I will blow this house down!" screamed the wolf.

Reader 2:

He puffed himself up to give his last big huff. That's when the old wolf burst with a bang.

Reader 1:

The little pigs heard the loud noise. They looked out. The wolf was gone!

Reader 2:

The pigs squealed with joy! They danced and sang. That night they slept very peacefully!

Reader 1:

The next morning the first two piglets built themselves new houses made with bricks and stones.

Glossary

encounter   to meet

piglet   a young pig

ruby   a gemstone that is purplish red in color

tantrum   a rage

The Turnip

Story Introduction

Adapted from a Brothers Grimm fairy tale, "The Turnip" is about a little old man and woman who grow a huge turnip. They alone cannot pull it out of the ground and ask for help from their friends. With the help of a small mouse, they learn that every person's contribution has value, no matter how small or weak one seems.

Reader 1:

The little old man loved to work in his garden.

Reader 2:

One day he saw a big turnip in his garden.

Reader 1:

"What a big turnip! I have never seen a turnip so big! It takes up a lot of space in my garden. I need to pull it up!" he said.

Reader 2:

He pulled at the top of the turnip. He pulled and pulled, but he could not pull the turnip up.

Reader 1:

Finally he called to his wife. "Wife, wife, come here! Help me! Help me! Help me, little old wife. Help me pull up this turnip."

Reader 2:

The little old wife ran over to help the little old man.

Reader 1:

The little old man pulled and pulled at the turnip. The little old wife pulled and pulled at the turnip.

Reader 1 and Reader 2:

They could not pull up the turnip.

Reader 2:

Along came a little girl named Amy.

Reader 1:

"Help! Help! Come here, little girl! We cannot pull up the turnip," cried the little old man and the little old wife.

Reader 2:

Amy ran to help. The little old man pulled at the turnip.

Reader 1:

The little old wife tugged at the little old man. The little girl named Amy tugged at the little old wife.

Reader 1 and Reader 2:

They could not pull up the turnip.

Reader 2:

"My dog will help!" cried the little girl named Amy.

Reader 1:

"But your dog cannot pull up the turnip!" said the little old man and his little old wife.

Reader 2:

Amy called her dog. The dog came running. His tongue was hanging out.

Reader 1:

His bushy tail was wagging. "Bow-wow, bow-wow," yelped the frisky dog. He was glad to help.

Reader 2:

The little old man pulled at the turnip. The little old wife tugged at the little old man.

Reader 1:
The little girl named Amy tugged at the little old wife. The frisky dog tugged at the little girl named Amy.

Reader 1 and Reader 2:
They could not pull up the turnip.

Reader 2:
"Little old wife, call your cat to help us!" said the little girl named Amy.

Reader 1:
"Here Kitty, Kitty! Come here my pretty Kitty!" called the little old wife.

Reader 2:
The tiger kitty ran quickly to the little old wife.

Reader 1:
"Meow, meow, meow, I can help!" purred the tiger kitty.

Reader 2:
The little old man pulled at the turnip. The little old wife tugged at the little old man. The little girl named Amy tugged at the little old wife.

Reader 1:
The frisky dog tugged at the little girl named Amy. The tiger cat tugged at the frisky dog.

Reader 1 and Reader 2:
They could not pull up the turnip.

Reader 2:
"We cannot pull this turnip up," said the little old wife.

Reader 1:
"You are right," said Amy. "We cannot pull up this turnip!"

Reader 2:
"What shall we do?" asked the little old man. "We cannot pull up this turnip."

Reader 1:

"Bow-wow! Bow-wow!" said the frisky dog. "Meow, meow, meow!" said the tiger cat.

Reader 2:

"I can help you!" said a tiny, gray mouse.

Reader 1:

The little old man, the little old wife, the little girl named Amy, the frisky dog, and the tiger cat were very surprised.

Reader 2:

The little old man pulled at the turnip. The little old wife tugged at the little old man. The little girl named Amy tugged at the little old wife.

Reader 1:

The frisky dog tugged at the little girl named Amy. The tiger cat tugged at the frisky dog. The tiny, gray mouse tugged at the tiger cat.

Reader 2:

They pulled and they pulled and they pulled.

Reader 1:

Finally, they all gave one last, big pull! And up came the turnip!

Glossary

contribution   something given in common with others

frisky   playful and full of energy

tug   to pull

turnip   the root of an edible herb

unearth   to dig up

From *Fairy Tales for Two Readers.* © 1995. Teacher Ideas Press. (800) 237-6124.

Appendix A: Guide to *Readability Level* of Stories

Readability levels are based on the Fry Readability Formula.

The Black Bull of Norroway	Reader 1 = 3.2	Reader 2 = 2.7
The Brave Little Tailor	Reader 1 = 1.8	Reader 2 = 2.2
Cap O' Rushes	Reader 1 = 2.2	Reader 2 = 1.5
Chicken Little	Reader 1 = 4.0	Reader 2 = 2.5
Clever Elsie	Reader 1 = 2.0	Reader 2 = 2.0
The Cunning Little Tailor	Reader 1 = 3.0	Reader 2 = 4.3
The Goose Girl	Reader 1 = 3.0	Reader 2 = 4.3
Kate Crackernuts	Reader 1 = 4.0	Reader 2 = 2.6
King Thrushbeard	Reader 1 = 3.6	Reader 2 = 3.3
Mother Holly	Reader 1 = 1.6	Reader 2 = 2.0
Mr. and Mrs. Vinegar	Reader 1 = 3.6	Reader 2 = 3.0
The Seven Ravens	Reader 1 = 2.3	Reader 2 = 1.6
The Six Servants	Reader 1 = 1.6	Reader 2 = 3.0
The Three Pigs	Reader 1 = 1.6	Reader 2 = 2.0
The Turnip	Reader 1 = 1.5	Reader 2 = 1.5

Appendix B:
Guide to
Oral Reading

Readers might like to consider the following about their own performances:

<u>Did I</u>

Enunciate (speak clearly) each word so that I could easily be understood?

Pronounce all words correctly?

Understand the meaning of all words, sentences, and paragraphs?

Group words in thought units—read in phrases?

Read smoothly, not stopping when there was no reason to stop?

Pay attention to punctuation marks?

Read neither too fast nor too slowly?

Keep my eyes ahead of my voice (i.e., practice good eye-voice span)?

Keep good eye contact with my audience and look away from my book momentarily?

Read with expression that helped my audience understand and enjoy what I read?

Enjoy what I read?

Know what the story was about when I finished reading?

Selected Bibliography

Andersen, Hans C. *Andersen's Fairy Tales.* Illustrated by Lisbeth Zwerger. Selected by Anthea Bell. Saxonville, MA: Picture Book Studio, 1992. $19.95pa. ISBN 0-88708-182-7.

Brett, Jan, reteller and illus. *Goldilocks and the Three Bears.* New York: Putnam, 1987. $13.95. ISBN 0-396-08925-9. Grades K-3.

Chase, Richard. *Grandfather Tales.* Boston: Houghton Mifflin, 1973. 240p. $13.95. ISBN 0-395-06692-1. Grades 4-6.

———. *The Jack Tales.* Boston: Houghton Mifflin, 1943. 207p. $13.95. ISBN 0-395-0694-8. Grades 4-6.

Climo, Shirley. *The Egyptian Cinderella.* Illustrated by Ruth Heller. New York: Thomas Y. Crowell, 1989. $13.98. ISBN 0-690-04824-6. Grades K-5.

Croll, Carolyn. *The Little Snowgirl.* New York: Putnam, 1989. 32p. $14.95. ISBN 0-399-21691-X. Grades PreK-K.

Dahl, Roald. *Roald Dahl's Revolting Rhymes.* New York: Alfred A. Knopf, 1983. 48p. $14.99; $14.00pa. ISBN 0-394-95422-X; 0-394-85422-5pa.; Grades 3-6.

dePaola, Tomie. *Tomie dePaola's Favorite Nursery Tales.* New York: Putnam, 1986. 127p. $17.95. ISBN 0-399-21258-2. Grades K-5.

Ehrlich, Amy. *The Random House Book of Fairy Tales.* New York: Random House, 1985. 223p. $17.00. ISBN 0-394-85693-7. Grades K-4.

Galdone, Paul. *The Elves and the Shoemaker.* New York: Clarion Books, 1986. 32p. $13.95. ISBN 0-89919-226-2. Grades PreK-3.

Rojankovsky, Feodor. *Tall Book of Nursery Tales.* New York: Alfred A. Knopf, 1944. 120p. $9.95. ISBN 0-06-025065-8. PreK-3.

Scieszka, Jon. *The Stinky Cheese Man and Other Fairly Stupid Tales.* New York: Viking, 1992. 56p. $16.00. ISBN 0-670-84487-X. Grades K-3.

————, reteller. *The True Story of the Three Little Pigs.* Illustrated by Lane Smith. New York: Viking, 1989. $13.95. ISBN 0-670-82759-2. Grades PreK-2.

Vuong, Lynette Dyer. *The Brocaded Slipper.* Illustrated by Vo-Dinh Mai. New York: HarperCollins Children's Books, 1992. 111p. $13.89. ISBN 0-397-32508-8. Grades 3 and above.

About the Authors

Betty L. Criscoe is a graduate of East Texas State University. She earned her degree in reading education from Syracuse University. A West Foundation Distinguished Professor of Education, Dr. Criscoe teaches courses in reading education and language arts at Midwestern State University, Wichita Falls, Texas. Dr. Criscoe has worked in Texas public schools as a classroom teacher of language arts subjects in grades four through nine and has received several teaching awards for her skill in the elementary, secondary, and college classrooms. In addition to writing articles on language arts subjects, Dr. Criscoe has co-authored a textbook in content reading. In 1991 the *School Library Journal* Reference Books Review Committee named her 1989 edition of *Award-Winning Books,* published by Scarecrow Press, one of the top thirty-one reference books of the year.

Philip J. Lanasa, III, is a graduate of Texas A&M University. He earned his M.L.S. Degree from the University of Oklahoma and his Ph.D. from Texas A&M. Dr. Lanasa is a West Foundation Distinguished Professor of Education at Midwestern State University in Wichita Falls, Texas. He has worked in Texas public schools as a teacher, school administrator, counselor, and special education diagnostician. He has also worked as director of two Houston museums. In addition to serving as a consultant and speaker on educational issues, he has worked as a member of the Southern Association Accreditation team. Dr. Lanasa's published works include two books, monographs, and articles on the subjects of multicultural education, computer science, bibliotherapy, and reading. His primary interests in the field of children's and young adult literature are in science fiction, fantasy, historical fiction, and biography.

Betty Criscoe and Phil Lanasa are a husband-and-wife team who consider their daughter, fifteen-year-old Amy, and their son, twelve-year-old John, to be among their greatest blessings.